BARE BONES

BARE BONES

I'M NOT LONELY IF YOU'RE READING THIS BOOK

BOBBY BONES

DEY ST.

AN IMPRINT OF WILLIAM MORROW PUBLISHERS

DEY ST.

The names and identifying characteristics of some of the individuals featured throughout this book have been changed to protect their privacy.

All insert photographs are courtesy of the author.

HarperCollins books may be purchased for educational, business, or sales promotional use. For information please e-mail the Special Markets Department at SPsales@harpercollins.com.

FIRST EDITION

Designed by Paula Russell Szafranski
Frontispiece photograph by Eddie Garcia

Library of Congress Cataloging-in-Publication Data has been applied for.

ISBN 978-0-06-241734-3

16 17 18 19 20 ᴏᴠ/ʀʀᴅ 10 9 8 7 6 5 4 3 2 1

For my grandma, my mom,

and everyone who ever took a chance on me

CONTENTS

Introduction: Or, Why We're All Here   IX

1 The Boy Behind the Ninja Turtle Mask   I

2 Nerd Alert   19

3 Smooth Operator   39

4 Country Mouse in the Big City   59

5 Stupid Panty Hose Tricks   73

6 Bones Bared   91

7 Fight. Grind. Repeat. And Sometimes Lose   107

8 Bones Goes Country   125

9 Gnawing at the Bones   145

10 A Total Nightmare   163

11 Every Day Is a Good Day   181

Acknowledgments   197

INTRODUCTION:
OR, WHY WE'RE ALL HERE

July 13, 2015

Right now, I am packing to fly to Los Angeles tomorrow, which is crazy. I'll tell you why.

But wait. First let me introduce myself.

Hi. I'm Bobby.

I do a radio show (a few of them, actually). It's really the only thing I'm good at. I have done a radio show basically every day of my life since I was a teenager. I don't like vacations. I don't even like weekends. I like to work. And to me, my work is talking on the radio. It's nice to meet you.

Okay, back to why I'm shoving my stuff in a bag to head out to the West Coast from Nashville, where I live.

About six months ago, I met up with a casting agent from one of the major networks while she was visiting Nashville, after a friend introduced us. We were talking about life and random stuff at the bar in her hotel. I really didn't know the importance of her job, which is what happens most of the time when I meet people in really high positions. Too dumb to know I should be networking, I just kind of stumble into things instead.

Three weeks after I met the casting agent, however, she sent me an e-mail inviting me to L.A. for a "meeting."

I've had "meetings" before, and most times they are just that, a meeting between you and someone else. You never get a job in that meeting; you rarely get a job *from* the meeting, either. But you go, because maybe, just maybe, something will come up later and that person you had the meeting with will remember you for it. That's Hollywood logic for you. (Something I'm still learning. I'm used to Arkansas logic—more on that later.)

So I flew four and a half hours to Los Angeles just to take the meeting, after which I planned to get on the first flight back to Nashville for a few hours of sleep before the usual 3 A.M. wakeup time for my morning radio show. It was going to be a pretty grueling couple of days, but when a TV network calls, you come a-runnin'.

As it turned out, the meeting wasn't just a meeting but a real live job prospect. "We're doing this show. Unfortunately I can't really tell you much about it, because we're keeping it under wraps," the casting agent said. "But we'd love for you to audition."

Hell, yeah!

I headed over to the studio where the auditions were being held. Now, I've interviewed for plenty of radio jobs, but I'd never been to a Hollywood audition. As soon as I entered a room filled with a bunch of great-looking people, I lost most of my hope of landing this gig. Listen, I'm a 6.2 at best on the 1-to-10 scale. But in Pretty People Land, where I was at that very moment, I immediately dropped to no better than a 3.8. There were models, reality stars, CNN anchors. And then there was me.

It didn't help my self-esteem any that I had worn jeans, a T-shirt, and tennis shoes when everyone else was in their Sunday best. I had no idea I was supposed to dress up! I am that clueless. As they say, you can take the boy out of Arkansas, but you can't take the Arkansas out of the boy.

In the middle of all this Los Angeles cool, that's exactly where I was catapulted back to: Mountain Pine, Arkansas, the tiny mill town where I grew up. At the audition, everyone, except me, seemed to know one another. The way they hugged and kissed hello, it was if they were all long-lost best friends at a high school reunion. Meanwhile I sat in the corner, staring out from under my baseball hat like a creep. I was right back at Mountain Pine School, the kid who ate lunch by himself in the corner of the cafeteria every day until graduation.

It was almost a relief when they called my name. Almost, because I had no idea what to expect when I sat down at a table with three other people.

The casting director said, "Talk about the current events of the day. Here, I'll get you started." She threw out a topic from the day's news and said, "Go!"

I might suck at socializing (and dressing, apparently), but if there's one thing that I'm good at, it's being quick on my feet. The two are related. When you're not popular as a kid, either you have to be funny or you'll routinely get the crap beaten out of you. I've built a career on the survival skill I honed early on: being a smart aleck who is good with a fast comeback.

So I sat there for two or three hours giving the ol' Bobby Bones take on everything from the Kardashians to global warming to the relative merits and demerits of Siri. Meanwhile, the casting director kept switching out the other two people on my panel. It was like the Hunger Games of television.

"Thank you. Your bags are here," they told the people asked to leave *every single time*. "We appreciate your time. You'll be escorted down."

It was excruciating. Whenever the casting agent stood up, I was just thinking, Uh-oh. Please don't stop at me. Please don't stop at me. Please don't stop at me. Please—oh, I made it. Ahhhhh.

By the time we broke for lunch, a hundred people had been whittled down to thirty-five. After lunch, it was right back to panel after panel after panel, and people getting cut and people getting cut. I'm not kidding. I felt like Katniss Everdeen fighting for her life. There were boy-band members—real-life, once massively famous boy-band members—who got cut right in front of me. Hunger Gamed out, their names went in the sky as they died. Meanwhile I kept getting pushed on and on until the day ended at 6 P.M. with six of us left. "We thought you did a great job," one of the casting agents said to me.

I couldn't believe it. I'd made it through. I was going to be on TV!

"We'd like to have you come back to the audition next week," the casting agent continued.

What! This wasn't the audition?

Turns out that this daylong death march was just the *start*, an early round to cut out the riffraff, which is exactly what I still was at that point (and still feel I am). So a week later, I was back on a Southwest flight from Nashville to L.A. This time, though, I showed up in a suit. I only put on a suit when it's time to go into battle.

I knew exactly what my game plan was this time. My job wasn't to be the funniest; my job wasn't to be the smartest; my job wasn't to be the most *anything*. Actually, that's not true: my job was to be the most human. While I can hold my own with great talents and have an opinion in the face of big personalities, I'm just a regular guy. I've accepted my position in life: that I'm never going to be that cool. And I'm okay with that.

Throughout my career—whether it's *The Bobby Bones Show* broadcasting across the country every morning on the radio for more than a decade, my comedy band Raging Idiots, or this TV show I was trying out for—I've always had the same voice, and I'm lucky to have it. Having grown up a trailer park kid on welfare and food stamps, becoming jaded is impossible. Although now I make a good living, which I'm not ashamed of; when you've been poor, it never leaves you.

Oh, wait. I'm gonna have to take a break from writing and continue this book later, because the person's here at my apartment for my spray tan.

PAUSE FOR SPRAY TAN. THANKS FOR YOUR PATIENCE.

I'm back. I get that it's funny to talk about how normal I am when a spray-tan person just left my place (that's why I put it in the book). Listen, I swear I wouldn't care about being spray-tanned or any kind of tan, but apparently you can't be pale on TV because the lights wash you out. Because I'm about to go be in front of the cameras for three days, I had to get spray-tanned. Don't judge me. Even though if, as a kid (when being tan wasn't a problem since we spent all our time outdoors without our shirts), I could have seen into the future and how much money I'd spend on getting a tan, I'd judge me, too.

So anyway, at the "real" audition for what I now knew was a new network talk show, I was going to sit at a table and just "be myself." And that's what I did. I wasn't spectacular, but I felt pretty solid, even though there were some big players like the Real Housewives. (And not the crappy ones. Apparently, there are two levels of Housewives. Who knew? There's, like, the Minor League Housewives who don't matter very much and the Big League Housewives who make bank.) During the audition, everyone was trying to get in the last word or the most words, in the hope of being noticed. Everyone but me.

Among all the famous faces talking around me, there was only one person who made me truly starstruck. I first spotted him when he sat down a few seats away from me during lunch. It was *the* greatest defensive back of all time: Florida State Seminole, All-American, and NFL Hall of Famer—that's right, I was sitting next to the one and only Prime Time! Deion Sanders!

I have always been a huge sports geek and did a national sports show for years. As a kid, I watched Deion in the NFL, and now . . . he was sitting right next to me. It was almost too much to believe. To make sure I had proof, I took some pictures of him while he wasn't looking and sent them to my friends (loser move, I know).

After I was done being a stalkerazzi I moved a few seats over so that I wasn't right next to him but a bit closer (I didn't want to be pushy). Although running through my head in a steady stream were the words, "I'm such a huge fan! I'm such a huge fan!" I played it cool.

"Hey, man. How you doing? I'm Bobby. Nice to meet you," I said to Deion freakin' Sanders.

"I'm Deion."

No kidding!

"Nice to meet you."

Then we continued to eat our very healthy meals, as we are both gentlemen who try to stay in shape. Really, he was the gentleman eating. I was just sitting there thinking, Don't stare too long. Don't stare too long. Don't stare too long. Okay, look. Okay, turn away! all the while texting all my friends, "I'm sitting next to Deion Sanders" or reporting on things I heard him saying to other people: "Deion just said this . . ."

With lunch over, it was time to be professional again. When I got my new panel, Deion was on it! He sat to the left, I sat to the right, and a random Housewife sat in the middle. Don't even remember who sat there, because I was in love with Deion.

We just clicked in that way people talk about when they find their soul mate (although I have no clue about that, actually, since I suck so bad at relationships with women, as you will soon read). Deion and I wound up working together for about five hours that day, much of it spent doing two-man panels. I thought we had formed a bond. But if I was at all unsure, what happened next made it irrefutable.

Deion and I were backstage talking when someone came around and offered us both a beer.

"No, thanks," he said. "I don't drink."

After refusing as well, I said, "I don't drink, either."

"Let me guess. Messed-up parents?"

"Yeah."

"I've never had a drink in my life."

"Me neither," I said.

In that very moment an ironclad bond was forged. It was clear that although we were from two very different worlds, we had experienced the same kind of struggles. Deion said he'd only ever met one other person who felt the same way about drinking. Neither one of us was morally against it; we'd just decided it wasn't for us, because of what we had seen it do to others.

We returned to the panels, and if we had chemistry before, we were killing it now. There was a new level of admiration and empathy between us. When he talked I just shut up, not because he was Prime Time, but because this was a dude who had been through tough circumstances. I totally related to and respected him—and wanted to hear what he had to say.

At the end of the day, after we'd been partnered up for hours, Deion Sanders said to me, "Let me give you my number."

"Hey, man. I'm never going to call you," I told him straight up. "So if I get your number, I'm just telling you now that I will never use it, because I would feel like I am bothering you."

But Deion put his number into my phone and said, "I want you to call me."

"I'm not going to."

Now I'm back in Nashville, packing—just zipped up the ol' garment bag, which I hate doing; I can't iron work crap, never could, and packing a garment bag means that something is going to need to be ironed—because I'm returning to L.A., where I'll see Deion again. This time, we were told, it's not an audition but a "chem test," meaning they are looking for people who work well with the two of us.

As excited as I am, I also know how the game works. This is a fickle business.

At any moment Johnny Seacrest, Ryan's long-lost brother, could show up and take the job. And that's just how you do. Even if he doesn't, there are still many obstacles between getting the job and having a TV show. The network has to agree to make the pilot; I have to do well on the pilot; the pilot has to be picked up to run on TV; then viewers have to tune in. The likelihood of me hosting a show with my new good buddy Deion Sanders is slim at best.

But the way I look at it, every day that I'm moving forward is a day I'm not moving backward. Just the fact that I'm in the race at all is a miracle. It's crazy that a kid who grew up on welfare in rural Arkansas, with a checked-out mom and no dad, is now someone who finds himself in the same room with network producers and an NFL great, even if I am too weirded out to call him.

Above my bed, I keep a picture of my hometown's road sign—MOUNTAIN PINE, POP. 772—as a constant reminder not only of where I come from and how much I've gone through to get where I am, but also of the kind of people I talk to on the radio every day. I try to help and entertain them with my show and my stories and hopefully this book. They are people just like me. I'll never forget that.

BARE BONES

1

THE BOY BEHIND THE NINJA TURTLE MASK

It sounds weird to say this, but I've almost died a bunch of times in my life. The first time I was five years old, running through the rain in the woods of Hot Springs, Arkansas.

Although I really spent most of my life in the nearby and much smaller town of Mountain Pine, on this fall afternoon in 1985, my mom, dad, little sister, and I were living in a house in Hot Springs. It was only temporary, though. We might have been there for a month.

I was being chased by my cousin. I say "cousin," but it was actually my mom's best friend's daughter, who we just called a cousin. That's a southern thing. And there were moments when we all lived together, so the idea of family wasn't such a stretch. Anyway, she was chasing me with a stick through the front lawn. Well, "lawn" isn't really accurate, either. In front of our house, there were a lot of woods, which is different. Rich people have lawns; country people have woods. So we had woods.

I ran up a ladder propped against the house and climbed onto the roof. No way was she going to get me up here. But up the ladder my cousin started, waving that stupid stick. Below me there was an old boat trailer. Why there was a boat trailer parked beside our house, in the woods, I have no idea. We didn't have a boat.

I moved to jump onto the grass. But my foot slipped on the rain-slicked roof and I did a belly flop right onto the base of the boat trailer. My stomach hurt so much I couldn't walk. My cousin scrambled down the ladder and lay down next to me in the wet grass. I wouldn't have slipped if it weren't for that damn rain! The same rain that rained out my first-ever Little League baseball game that my dad had signed me up for. That was where I was supposed to be, instead of getting chased around by my cousin with a stupid stick.

I didn't know any better, so like any dumb kid who grew up in Arkansas, I stayed outside and tried to ignore that I was hurt. Finally I got up and limped into the house and didn't think much about it. But my stomachache got so bad through the rest of the day and night that I couldn't eat or sleep. And it was hard to breathe. Where we came from, though, you didn't just go to the doctor. That's a poor-person mentality that basically comes from the fact that doctor visits are expensive without insurance (and one I still have today, even though I now have great health insurance). The medical protocol for poor people is: If something hurts, get over it. If something hurts real bad, put salve on it. Something has to hurt real, *real* bad to merit a trip to any kind of fancy-pants doctor. And forget about the dentist—I didn't step into one of those guys' offices until I was in my twenties (and I'm still paying for that).

The day after my fall onto the boat trailer, my breathing became even more labored. That's when my mom decided to take me to the hospital. I had only seen the inside of a hospital on TV. So although I was in terrible pain, getting to walk into an actual hospital with real doctors was exciting enough for me to forget about my injury for a moment. However, in the emergency room the pain returned and was so bad that I couldn't walk anymore. All the novelty wore off. A nurse rushed toward me with a wheelchair, which she immediately rolled into an examination room where people in white coats did whatever they do with X-rays and other big machines. Even at that age, I knew something bad was going on. It all ended when a doctor said to my mom, "We've got to get him into surgery immediately." While a mask was slapped on my face, my mom began to cry. I passed out immediately. (I'm still a total lightweight to this day; a dose of NyQuil and it's like I've been hit by a tranquilizer gun.)

When I woke up hours later, there were people all around me. There was my mom by my head and my grandmother at my feet. But all along the perimeter of the hospital bed were people from our church. My grandma, my mom's mom, had us going to the First Pentecostal Church of Jessieville, another small town in Garland County, where Hot Springs and Mountain Pine are located. The older, mostly female congregants around my bed were all friends of my grandmother's. There was a lot of prayer. And a lot of love.

I had undergone emergency surgery to remove a ruptured spleen and wound up spending eight days recovering in the hospital. A deep, ugly scar ran from beneath my belt line all the way to the bottom of my sternum. But I was lucky. The doctor told my mom that if I had gone untreated for six more hours, I would have drowned internally in my own blood. At the time, I took it all as no big deal. But looking back now, I think, *Holy crap,* I almost died from my insides bleeding. I was pretty lucky, and also pretty stupid not to have let my mother know a little sooner how much pain I felt. If this had happened when I was twenty-five, I surely could have used the story to impress girls, right?

Falling on the boat trailer and the surgery after is the earliest complete memory I have. While some of my friends say they can remember things like coming out of their mother's vagina and into the light, I think that's a load of crap. (And not only do I not believe them, I don't like stories about my mom's vagina even if true.) But the events of that day and following week stand out clearly in my mind not just because I could have died or because I got to stay in the hospital or was the center of attention for a while—but because that was also the last time in my life that I felt like I had a dad. Whether there was any connection between my getting hurt and my biological father going peace-out, I have no clue. All I know is this: we were a family, I landed in the hospital, and when I got out he was gone for good.

At least that's how I remember it. Right at the age my memories started to come into focus, he faded out. Still, I know a few things about him—like how he got my mom pregnant when she was fifteen years old.

Although my mother, Pam Hurt, was originally from Kansas City, Missouri, she moved during her teenage years to Arkansas, where my dad, who was two years older than her, was from. The youngest of four siblings, my mom was best friends with her sister Cindy. In high school, they ran together in a group of kids that included my biological father and his brother.

Whenever I tell people that I'm from Arkansas and I have "double cousins," they assume I'm talking about incest. (Shout-out to Arkansas stereotypes! For the record, I have never dated any of my cousins. Only made out.) What happened was my mom married my dad (I'm assuming because she got pregnant), and my aunt Cindy married my dad's brother Rick Estell. So my cousins, Mary and Josh, and my sister and I have the same two sets of grandparents. My uncle Rick, a wonderful guy with his own roofing, landscaping, and other businesses, was a solid influence on me while I was growing up—and the exact opposite of my dad, who vanished from my life.

I had no idea where or why my dad went and wasn't made to understand what happened. I didn't know what questions to ask when I was young; and then I was too resentful to ask them when I was older. But I decided that I wasn't missing anything. The only memory I have of him from before he left is a hazy image of being in a room with him and a bunch of other guys. He was trying to get me to say curse words in front of his buddies—I guess he thought it would be funny to hear a four-year-old drop the F-bomb—but I wouldn't do it. I was a prude even then. Pretty dumb memory, I know.

Once I got out of the hospital, my family became my mother and little sister, Amanda, who was four years younger than me. My sister and I were close in that way you are with someone you live with in a very small house. I tried to be a good older brother and protect her (not that I was a tough kid by any stretch; I was a huge nerd and wimp and quite small). But we weren't best friends or anything. Four years is quite the age difference when you are kids, especially when you are a boy and girl.

With my dad gone, we moved in with my grandmother into her trailer at the top of the big hill in Jessieville. Soon after that, the four of us moved to an apartment in Mountain Pine. Mountain Pine, Jessieville, and Hot Springs are all neighboring communities within a twenty-minute radius of each other, but only Hot Springs, with a population of about thirty thousand people, was "town." So if you had to go to Walmart to get washing powders, or get groceries from the Piggly Wiggly or Sunny Delight from Food 4 Less, you would go into Hot Springs. (I particularly loved Sunny Delight and just assumed it was orange juice. It wasn't until years later that I found out there's a huge difference between orange juice and orange *drink*. But when I was a kid, SunnyD was a huge treat at our house. I would pour half of a new bottle into an empty SunnyD bottle, and then fill them both up with water. This way I managed to have two bottles of Sunny Delight for the price of one. Bobby: 1; being poor: 0.)

Mountain Pine, population seven hundred, was segregated when I grew up there and is still that way today. The black and white neighborhoods are actually divided right down the middle of what was once a company mill town. Dierks Lumber and Coal Company, which began producing lumber there in the 1920s, owned all the homes and commercial property, like the movie theater and hotel, through the 1960s. But Dierks eventually sold the mill to Weyerhaeuser, which, after years of layoffs, finally closed it in 2006—putting nearly half the town out of work.

Mountain Pine is a pretty town to look at, and I had a lot of fun growing up there. But it was a pretty impoverished place. I don't actually remember a movie theater or hotel, even though the Internet tells me they were there. All I remember is the Yum Yum shop, with a broken pool table, and Parthenas general store, where we used food stamps to buy hamburgers.

We made fun however we could. My buddy Scotty had the town Nintendo, meaning he was the only one in Mountain Pine who could afford the video game console. So we'd all gather at Scotty's and jockey to get into games of Tecmo Bowl or Double Dribble. Scotty was the man because of that! And he remains one of my dear friends to this day. Mostly because he still has a Nintendo.

I was a trailer kid for a lot of my life. But I lived in very few trailer parks. In trailer parks, where there can be thirty trailers crammed in beside each other on fifteen lots, everyone is in each other's business, for good and bad. When you don't have much, you need people more but trust them even less, and because of this trailer parks can have more drama than a Lifetime movie. But we weren't trailer park people; we were single-trailer-in-the-woods people. Like with lawns vs. woods, there's a difference—and it's price. Renting a trailer in the woods is cheaper. We had to do anything we could to save a buck, since our main source of income was my mom's welfare and my grandma's Social Security check. Those who the talking heads on the news called "leeches on America," that was us.

My mom struggled. A high school dropout, she turned sixteen on March 8, 1980, and gave birth to me on April 2. How could she have done anything other than struggle? When I was little, she bounced around from job to job, never working anywhere more than part-time and never long term. She did a brief stint at a rent-to-own store, a concept many readers might not be familiar with unless they grew up broke like me. Let me take a minute to explain. When you want something, like a TV, but can't afford said TV, you can use layaway (which we did a lot). You pay it off with no interest but only get the TV when you finish paying. With rent-to-own, you get the TV, but—there's always a but—there's a heavy interest tacked on top of the original price. So you're basically renting until you own it (or the store takes it back). She didn't last there too long. I think being around all these things she couldn't have just bummed her out.

Mom also waited tables for a while at Hunan's, a local Chinese restaurant. The biggest perk of the job was that I had free Mongolian beef every Thursday, Friday, and Saturday night for about a year. That was the longest time I remember her holding a job. Usually they only lasted for a couple of weeks and then she'd get fired or quit.

Like the Mongolian beef that was my main source of nutrition for a good thirteen months, if something was there for free, we got it. At Christmas, other families from the local church would drop off boxes of donations at our trailer, apartment, or wherever we were living, so that we would have gifts for the holiday. I knew it was charity, but it didn't bother me. Not yet realizing that people felt sorry for me, I was just happy to get a present.

What did bother me, though, was watching my mom steal food when we went grocery shopping. I dreaded going to the Piggly Wiggly or Food 4 Less because I knew at some point Mom was going to have to take out the heap of brightly colored construction paper they called food stamps back then. Now, when you receive welfare benefits you swipe a card that looks like a credit or debit card. Back then we used to have to peel off big pieces of yellow, purple, or red paper, representing different denominations, which could be seen from a mile away. We were basically screaming, "Here we are with our construction paper money. That's right, we're poor!" Counting off the stamps at the cash register was humiliating. But food stamps meant food, and you had to take what you could get. Like I always say, "Gotta eat."

Unfortunately I guess the stamps weren't enough, because my mom also stole. In her own take on the Supplemental Nutritional Assistance Program, I watched her go into a section where there weren't any people (i.e., not the deli counter, where there was always somebody around). After looking left and right—her small dark features scanning the aisles from under her curly dark hair to make sure the coast was clear—she grabbed an item and slipped it into her purse and then a few more into the American flag leather jacket she hardly ever took off. There was no getting dressed up for things where we came from. When I was a kid, getting dressed up meant your jeans weren't dirty and your shirt had a button somewhere on it. But my mom was sure proud of that red, white, and blue leather jacket. I loved it, too. It was leather. And American. What could be cooler than that?

It also provided the perfect hiding place for the one or two grocery items she carried unnoticed out of the store on her petite frame. Usually she took nonperishable stuff, canned food, like Manwich. My mom would steal a lot of Manwich.

If you don't know what Manwich is this might not be the book for you, but if you're curious, google it. While I was growing up, it was basically one of the food groups, which in my house were as follows:

- ♪ Generic brands of cereal, such as Fruit Hoops (not Froot Loops) and Honey Squares (not Honeycomb)
- ♪ Manwich, which covered our protein intake

♪   Sunny Delight

♪   And white bread. Lots of white bread. White bread
     with mustard was a mustard sandwich, and they were
     good.

Back to my mom: I was so mad at her, because she was stealing. And we were taught stealing was wrong. But I never said
anything to her about this. I'm pretty sure she knew I knew what
she did, but she never talked about it with me, either. Instead, she
loaded the groceries into the car, turned on the radio, and drove
home.

The issue was, I knew Mom didn't steal for fun. The issue
was far more complicated than a simple case of right and wrong.
Yes, stealing was bad. I learned that at school, at church, on TV.
Yet even I could understand that welfare only went so far. If she
didn't take those things from the store, my sister, grandma, and
I wouldn't have enough to eat. Was it wrong to steal if it was to
feed your family? I wasn't sure. It was confusing.

I wondered if other kids' parents stole. Trying to make sense
of this moral gray zone, I asked a friend at school, "Does your
mom ever try to sneak stuff out of the grocery store?" He thought
I was kidding. Or maybe he didn't and was trying to hide his
embarrassment for me. Either way, the fact that what my mom
was doing was not the norm was an awful realization.

The shame I felt in that moment outpaced anything I experienced watching my mom shove a Velveeta down her pants. My
mom might have been doing what she needed to in order to get
by, but it still wasn't what ordinary folks did. I never asked anyone about that again.

To her credit, I never saw my mother steal anything that we

didn't need. By that I mean she wasn't stealing alcohol. And, trust me, she had awful issues with alcohol.

On occasion, she came home really drunk and stumbled around. But mostly she took her medicine in a slow drip. Most every night she sat in her chair in the living room, watching her shows and drinking a twelve-pack of Busch. I know because I never had a bedroom in any of the places we lived, so I used to sleep on the living room couch, where things were always happening around me, mostly my mom drinking night after night until she passed out in front of the television. After I was done with my homework and ready to go to bed, I'd change into my pajamas (read: shorts) from the "closet" under my bed where I kept all my clothes and take the sheets and comforter that I had folded up and crammed beside the couch in the morning to make up my bed. Then I'd fall asleep to the TV blaring (which is why to this very day I can't sleep without it). In the morning when I got up for school, sometimes my mom was still there in that chair, sometimes not.

It might seem depressing reading this now. Hell, it's kind of depressing to write it. But at the time, it was just everyday. In some sort of twisted version of a lullaby, I didn't mind drifting off to *The Golden Girls* or *Roseanne,* punctuated by the occasional pop of another Busch being cracked open. That was how I knew my mom. My mom struggled, but I loved her. The tricky part was gauging her moods. In other words, I never knew what kind of mood she would be in, ever. There were some times when she came home from wherever she'd been smiling and singing (she could actually sing pretty well and loved to do it; I didn't get that gene). She'd give me a hug and I knew the world was a fine place.

Just as often, though, the world was terrible, and during those times my mom was dark and sullen. She would lock down, showing no emotion and refusing to interact with anyone. If you tried to talk to her, she would snap and get angry for no apparent reason until she eventually disappeared into her bedroom. This was a time before bipolar existed, or at least before people in Arkansas knew it existed. When you have trouble paying for shoes, you don't have the expendable income to spend on a therapist.

I never knew what precipitated her bad moods. It wasn't like she sunk into them because she lost a job, had a fight with a friend, or anything else specific. They seemed to come and go without warning and be completely out of her control. I never trusted that I knew what or how my mom was feeling. So I figured I would control the only thing I could: myself. If she wasn't in a good place, I made sure to stay out of the way. During those times I didn't talk to her at all because she got angry quickly. And because I never could trust or predict what mood she would be in, I really didn't engage with my mom much in general.

All I wanted to do was stay out of the way, shove any traces of my existence into hidden corners like I did my sheets and comforter beside my couch. My mom had enough problems without me adding to them. And the best way for me to take up as little space or attention at home as possible was to be alone. I started doing everything by myself as soon as I could get around and was smart enough to figure out how. I rode my bike to school starting in second grade, played by myself, did my homework alone, and put myself to bed.

Keeping to myself was imprinted on me at a very young age. My mom and I hardly ever talked. I mean we had normal superficial exchanges like "How was your day?" "Good," but nothing deeper than that. I can't remember ever having a single serious or real conversation with my mom my entire childhood. Not the girl talk, bully warnings, or the do-good-in-school speech. Nothing. I don't blame her for it; in fact I liked it that way. But the fallout is that I'm terrible at having normal relationships now. And I'm not talking just about romantic ones (although I'm not exactly a superstar in that arena). Like playing a musical instrument or riding a bike, I never got good at communicating because I never did it as a kid.

Although no one would accuse me of being a people person and I still do most things by myself, I probably wouldn't have been able to forge any kind of human connection if it hadn't been for my grandmother, Hazel Hurt.

My grandmother, a small, heavyset woman, was my dad and mom, both. If I had any sort of stable environment whatsoever, she was the one who provided it. Although she never remarried after my grandfather died of cancer, when my mom was around eight years old, my grandmother had plenty of friends. Loud and outgoing, she was even friends with Virginia Clinton, Bill Clinton's mom, while they were neighbors in the same Hot Springs apartment complex. Even though I would never have called my mom political, I have a photo of her and the future president from when she volunteered for his campaign to become governor of Arkansas. I played with Chelsea quite a bit at Virginia's when we were little kids, so I've been told.

Grandma made an impression wherever she went. She sometimes led services at the Pentecostal church she took me to as a young kid, playing the guitar and singing along. She loved music—particular the classic giants of country music like Johnny Cash and Conway Twitty. One of her all-time favorites was

Randy Travis. We would sit and listen to old records constantly—
and play cards.

My grandmother taught me how to play cards, count cards in
a single deck, and even cheat at cards. She would play an Andy
Griffith gospel album or even Ray Charles while we played five-
card draw or in-between well into the night. Then, after a full
night of music and gambling, we would leave before the sun rose
to head out to the yard sales if it wasn't a Sunday.

From my grandmother I learned to master the art of the yard
sale. You lay out your map of sales, circle and number them in
order of possibility for good hauls, and make sure you're at the
best one the earliest. You had to be at the most promising ones
at the crack of dawn or all the good stuff would already be gone,
because there were a lot of other people just like us who had been
waiting all night to get deals on furniture, lamps, clothes, toys,
and other things we couldn't afford in a store. Grandma was
always on the hunt for religious paraphernalia, like crosses and
Jesus figures. Me? I just wanted shoes that fit. The first pair of Air
Jordans I ever owned were scored from a yard sale.

Music and poker and yard sales, that's what we did. Yeah, my
grandma and I had some good times. She wasn't a strict discipli-
narian (no one in our neck of the woods was), but she provided
the stability I needed and lots of love. There were the late-night
card games and early-morning rummage sales, but she also
hugged me and said she loved me all the time.

Of all her children and grandchildren, I was the one closest to
my grandmother. We even slept in the same bed for a while. In
the place we lived when I was in elementary school, my sister and
mother shared one bedroom while my grandmother and I shared
another. We were that close.

It was years later, though, that I found out my grandmother had actually officially adopted me. I only discovered the fact when I saw a Social Security card on her dresser that said Bobby Hurt as opposed to my father's name, Estell. I was twelve, old enough to understand it but still confused why she had done it and why I was never told. When I asked her to explain she said, "I had to be your legal guardian for a while because your mom was gone." And that was the end of the conversation. As much as my grandma loved me, she wasn't going to share those painful details. To this day I still don't know why she did what she did, or where my mother went when she left. She clearly didn't want me to know, because at some point my legal name was changed back to its original—Bobby Estell, which it remains today.

I wasn't going to bother my poor grandmother, who let me sleep in her bed and kept a roof over our heads thanks to her Social Security checks, with a bunch of uncomfortable questions. I worried enough that it was hard for her to have a calm and peaceful life because she was forced to raise me and my sister. I didn't want to make her life any more difficult. That worry was part of a larger anxiety I couldn't shake, the sense that I shouldn't be here at all, that I was a mistake. Maybe it was an overblown sense of self, but I felt responsible for my family's problems. It started with my mom, who was never able to have a real life, because when you get pregnant at fifteen years old, how great are things going to get for you? In my book, she never had a shot.

I felt guilty that my mom was stuck with me. When I first learned about adoption the way any little kid might (sitting in church, listening to adults talk), I wondered, Why didn't Mom do that? The thought wasn't marked by sadness or even judgment. It was just a logical question stemming from my surprise that she kept me. My guilt wasn't consuming but a low-level irritation, like a small rock hidden somewhere in my shoe. It stuck with me my whole childhood, even through what were supposed to be good times, like my tenth birthday party.

I didn't have a lot of birthday parties growing up for a couple of different reasons. The first was the money issue. When your mom is stealing Manwich, there usually isn't cash lying around to rent a bouncy castle. (Money, you'll see, is a recurring topic in this book, and at some point in reading, I'll understand if you yell at these pages, "WE GET IT, YOU WERE POOR!" But roll with me. It's my book. And if you tell your friends about it, and they buy it . . . I'll be even less poor!) My mom would always acknowledge my birthday with some kind of small celebration—usually just a cake. But when I turned ten it was a big deal to her, and she decided she wanted to do something special.

In the days leading up to the big party (a theme party: Teenage Mutant Ninja Turtles), she was excited in a way I hadn't seen before. Returning from the Dollar Store, where she'd gone on a major shopping spree, she unloaded bags with Teenage Mutant Ninja Turtle masks, birthday candles, paper plates, and napkins. She had also bought a mini wading pool and a bunch of plastic water guns.

All the fuss seemed crazy to me, but Mom talked about how important it was that I was turning ten. "Double digits," she said. "You're hitting double digits." What did that even mean? That I was old enough to take care of myself? Maybe.

The party was held outside the Hot Springs house we were staying in with my grandma and a couple of cousins and was everything a birthday party is supposed to be. Food, cake, kids (mostly more cousins), water fights, balloons, and my mom running around and having fun. I was happy she was happy. But the party didn't make me feel special; it made me uncomfortable.

I don't mind birthdays as a concept. I don't mind getting older. But I hate birthday *parties*—at least ones for me. Other people's parties are fine. I'm just not a big fan of any sort of thing honoring me. Dinners, breakfasts, whatever; I don't like celebrations of me. I worry that people feel forced to attend ("We have to go; it's his *birthday*"), and I never want to be the one causing others to feel uncomfortable. I would rather do nothing than ask people to go out of their way for me.

That's how I feel now and that's how I felt when I turned double digits. Even as I watched a boy from down the road stuff cake in his face and my sister spray the weeds with a water gun, I was sure I was putting everyone out. Not to mention the fact that my mom must have spent every dime she had and didn't have in order to throw this party. The only part I liked was the green Teenage Mutant Ninja Turtle mask that I could hide behind. (Cue sad music.)

If I was going to be the center of attention—something I wasn't against and actually really wanted—I was going to have to earn it.

2

NERD ALERT

Though my dad was MIA, there were father figures in my life who I am really grateful for.

Although at times our biological dad lived only a few miles away, my mom, sister, and I never had contact with him again after he left. He came and went from Arkansas, moving around from state to state. I would occasionally visit his side of the family who lived over by Buckthorn Road, which snaked all the way up a big, densely wooded mountain. But not if he was in town.

How I knew he was there or not, I have no clue, because I never, ever mentioned him to anyone in my family and they showed me the same courtesy. I did such a good job of acting as if I had no interest in him that even I believed it. I didn't want to be known as the kid who cared about his dad when his dad didn't care about him. I'm sure there was a part of me that was curious about him, but there was no way I would ever give him the satisfaction of knowing that.

Some kind of force field developed where even in a town of seven hundred people and a family that included double cousins, my dad and I were able to completely avoid each other. It wasn't unlike in college, when after I'd gotten a girl to go on a date with me, she'd somehow avoid me for the rest of the semester even though it was only a campus of a few thousand students.

Only once, when I was thirteen, did I run into my dad. I had been at my best friend (to be honest, my only real school friend) Evan McGrew's house. There was a gas station/convenience store right next door. I had gone there for a soda, and when I walked in, there *he* was. It was as if I had seen an alien. I have no idea if he saw me or not, because I immediately ducked behind a shelf of candy bars and snuck out the front. He certainly didn't follow me out or anything—I doubt he saw me, and if he did, he surely wouldn't have cared.

My heart was thumping, though. It had been about eight years since I'd last seen his face. Anxiety overtook me in the moment, followed quickly by anger. I'm sure underneath it all was sadness. Now, I see that. But at the time I responded by making a dash for Evan's, where I explained the fact that I had returned without any soda as my simply having changed my mind. I avoided confrontation like the plague. While I was willing to leave my actual father behind in the aisle of a convenience store without a word, I still wanted some kind of dad in my life. So I sought out father figures where I could. Luckily, a few kind guys took the bait.

Church was an easy place to look. Mountain Pine was a very religious place. Church was important to me because I needed somewhere to go, somewhere to have a group and fit in. I didn't really have religious feelings; I believed what I was taught to believe. My grandmother had taken us when we were young. When I was old enough, I took myself, not out of love for Christ but because I wanted to be around adults who were consistent and cared. I knew by going to church I would stay out of trouble. I knew what I didn't want, which was to wind up like my mom: a teenage parent with no shot at a future. I enjoyed school, but they don't really let you stay there much past 3 P.M. I needed a positive place where I could get some sort of guidance, so church was the best bet.

For me that place was Mountain Pine Baptist Church, where I spent Sunday mornings and nights and Wednesday afternoons as a member of the youth group. During summer I attended church camp, and later, in high school, I was president of the Fellowship of Christian Athletes. I didn't go to that church because of my family. My grandma kept attending her Pentecostal church. Mom's church had become that chair in front of the television. I went to church by myself, mainly drawn to Mountain Pine Baptist because of its location (five blocks away from where we lived) and its youth director, Robert Parker, who was a great influence on me and many of my friends. He influenced us not by having one-on-one talks with us about anything deep but by taking us places. Whenever I was with him there were always a few other kids around at least, and we did all kinds of things from hunting to rodeos. I went to my first-ever concert with him when we went to see the Christian country band Diamond Rio.

We also hung out at his house all the time. Robert and his wife, Missy, would gather a lot of us from the area and invite us to stay at their home Saturday nights, so they could make sure we were at church on Sunday morning. Those nights were filled with movies and board games until we passed out in the sleeping bags they had thrown on the floor for us. Sunday mornings meant a full breakfast and lots of laughs around the table. Through Robert and Missy, I got a taste of the kind of home life I had only dreamed about.

Fans of my show are familiar with Vic Gandolph, who was my football coach from the eighth grade until I graduated high school. He still calls in to the show, and to be honest I'm not even sure I'd have a show without him. I know it seems hard to believe, but I was really dedicated to playing football, despite being a scrawny pip-squeak compared to most of the team. Coach Gandolph taught me to own up to your mistakes and that a lot of people have talent, but talent alone doesn't win. "If you want to win," he said, "you must outwork everyone else, every day, all the time." It's very much where my "Fight. Grind. Repeat." mantra came from. He also taught me about adversity—that it's not *if* we face it but how we react *when* we face it. "Tough times don't last," he said, "but tough people do." I'm so grateful for my relationship with this man.

Then there was my best friend Evan's dad, Jerry McGrew. Evan and I had bonded over baseball; we were both on the team and Jerry was the coach. I admired Jerry, a veteran, because he had been injured in combat and still kept such a positive outlook on life. He also loved coaching Evan and me, even though Evan was his son and far more talented than I was. But I worked harder. And I think Jerry respected that. The McGrews also took me on my only childhood vacation. We went on a van trip to Colorado. I don't know if I had ever even been out of Arkansas at that point, and for sure my family couldn't afford any kind of vacation. But they took me to the mountains and paid for everything. I'm not kidding when I say that it is still one of the highlights of my life, and something I am still incredibly grateful for.

But by far the most significant stand-in I had for a father was my stepdad, Keith. I got lucky as a teenager; my mom married a good guy.

When I was about thirteen years old, we moved into his house and instantly made it very, very crowded. There were six of us at one time in his nine-hundred-square-foot place: my mom, stepdad, his two daughters, my sister, and me. So, again, I slept on the living room couch, cramming my bedding behind it and my clothes underneath.

But for the next four years, until I left for college, Keith was a solid and consistent presence—meaning, he had a job. My stepdad worked at the mill, when there still was one. Although he worked a lot, he still found time to do those things that I had heard fathers were supposed to.

He played catch with me in the backyard and even let me play on his adult softball team, which as a young kid was a blast. He was a decent athlete, but his real passion was fishing, and he often took me with him. I had fantasized about fishing with my dad, but when the time came to do the real thing I found it pretty darn boring. It didn't matter, though. Anytime Keith asked if I wanted to go fishing, I said yes, because I just wanted that father-son experience. We hunted, too, which I wasn't into. I don't like to kill animals, even though I like to eat them. (I recognize the hypocrisy of my statement. The deer we killed were good, and so was the pork I ate a few minutes ago.)

I was surprised whenever my stepdad showed up at one of my baseball games. I don't think anyone else from my family ever came to one of my school or sporting events, which I used as a form of permission to try whatever I wanted to as opposed to as a reason to hold myself back. I was never told that I could do things, but I was also never told that I couldn't.

Still, I had to admit it was nice seeing Keith in the stands that day, particularly since he had a job and therefore a good excuse for not being able to come to any of my games. I didn't make a big deal of it, and neither did he, but I liked it when he was there.

Despite every sign that proved Keith was a reliable man, when it came down to it, I never truly believed he would be there forever. I liked the idea of having a dad, but I didn't trust my mom to keep him around. I had no idea what their relationship was about. From my position, it was pretty dysfunctional. He worked a lot, and she sat home a lot drinking. My mom was who she was, and she was never going to change. Sadly, I too was hardwired by the time Keith came into our lives. I liked having him around, but as a teenager I'd already been burned enough by adults not to trust anyone but myself.

My mentality was very much that I was on my own, something that was reinforced by the fact that I had zero rules as a kid. I could do what I wanted, go where I wanted, see whom I wanted. As long I was on my couch/bed by eleven o'clock (and really, no one would notice if I *wasn't* there by eleven), there weren't any questions. You'd think as the kid with no rules I'd have some pretty cool partying stories. But I have none. I was and still am what most would consider a loser socially. I spend a lot of time alone. Even today my dog gets annoyed at me that we don't leave my bedroom.

The flipside of all of this freedom was that I didn't have anyone pushing me along, either. If anything was going to happen in my life, I knew I was going to have to be the one to put that into motion.

I was a really overachieving little kid, but not because I thought I had to be better than anyone else. Actually, it was just the opposite. Because there was no one to tell me I was any good at all, I worked hard to be the best so that there was no question I was good. This was particularly true at school. I was completely petrified of ending up like my mom and knew from enough after-school specials that if I didn't get an education, that's exactly where I'd wind up. (Yes, everyone below the age of twenty-five years old reading this, there used to be TV shows aimed at kids that included a heartfelt message. And they showed them at a specific time after school. I ate them up like Count Chocula cereal.)

Whether in school or out, I was super focused. I was lucky to have some natural ability when it came to academics. I was always able to pick things up quickly. That's not to say I coasted through junior high and high school. I also worked very hard, because I enjoyed studying and learning. By working hard in school I knew I could get past the railroad tracks that led out of our town, and that is what I wanted to do. As my buddy Evan wrote in one of my high school yearbooks, "Those railroad tracks may only be four feet wide, but they are almost impossible to cross."

One example of my push to learn as much as I could is my encyclopedia habit. Beginning at nine years old, I would save up all my money from mowing yards, raking leaves, and any other odd jobs I could get ("allowance" was only a word on TV, and I hated the kids who got allowance on TV. Those kids on *Who's the Boss?* always pissed me off! And don't get me started on *Mr. Belvedere*). As soon as I had enough saved from my work around Mountain Pine, I'd get a ride from my grandma into town to go to the Piggly Wiggly, where I could buy an encyclopedia. Starting with Androphagi, I spent the next six years buying volumes of the encyclopedia, reading them front to back and building a wall out of them in whatever house we lived in at the time, until I wound up at Zymotic. For the record, I don't know if it was really Androphagi or Zymotic. I seriously just looked those two words up to seem cool. I could have easily said A to Z.

But I read the full set the way kids today read *Harry Potter*. Or kids five years ago read *Harry Potter*. I don't think kids read anymore. They watch YouTube videos. My buddy Eddie has a two-year-old who will spend an hour watching YouTube videos of a guy opening plastic eggs. Finding out what is inside each egg is the entertainment. Sounds dumb, but I watched a few and was totally hooked. Then I watched ten straight minutes of some weird dude with pale hands opening up plastic eggs that contained everything from candy to a Lego. Good thing YouTube wasn't around back when I was a kid or I never would have learned a thing. Speaking of which, I may take a break and go watch those egg videos for a bit. You should do it, too. Trust me, at first you'll think, This is stupid and meant for a two-year-old. But fifteen minutes later you'll be saying, "Just one more."

Back to the encyclopedia—my grandma got a real kick out of it. "Look at you!" she said one day when I returned from the grocery store with Volume 22, Islam to Life. "You got your next encyclopedia!" (I made up Islam to Life, too. But you get the idea.)

Always real supportive of my learning, my grandma started

to give me a dollar for every A on my report card. But when report cards came out, I would have eight subjects and eight A's, which meant eight bucks. That was a lot of money in our house. Eventually, my grandma said, "I can't afford it anymore." She had to lower the payment to a dollar per report card. The money was nice, but more than that I loved the acknowledgment that I had done a good job. I worked hard for those A's, and like I said, in my family people were focused on getting food on the table. There weren't a lot of pats on the back to go around, though I know my grandmother meant well.

Everything—getting A's or reading encyclopedias—fed into a great desire I felt to be in competition with the world. I understood that to get out of Mountain Pine I had to rise to the top in some way. I don't remember when I first knew I had to get out of my hometown; that goal just always seemed to be a part of me. But as I got older, certainly by high school, it was obvious that very few opportunities existed in the place where I grew up. I didn't have any money or status, even in Mountain Pine, so the only way I was going to differentiate myself was by working hard and knowing more than other students. As soon as I realized that, life became a competition. I think it was probably a one-sided competition, but I didn't care.

That competitive drive is what catapulted me to become captain of the twelfth-grade Quiz Bowl team when I was only a seventh grader. As a twelve-year-old on the senior team, I was a shrimp among giants. But I was pretty good. Nah, I was great! And I got sooooo many girls by being the captain of the Quiz Bowl team in seventh grade. Walking down the hall at school, I had my pick of the ladies. I was THE MAN. Okay, that's a total lie. I'd say that being the captain of the Quiz Bowl team for five years straight probably contributed to the fact that I was a virgin into my twenties.

The competitions pitted one school team against another, and the matches were similar to *Jeopardy!* With four people on each team, you hit a buzzer if you knew the answer to questions on a wide range of subjects such as science, history, sports, current events, you name it. Contestants didn't even need to wait for the end of the question to be read before hitting the buzzer, which added another layer of stress to the game. But that's where I was awesome. No one was faster than me. (Unfortunately, sometimes I'm still quick but not in a good way, if you know what I mean.)

There were Quiz Bowl teams for every grade level from elementary school all the way up to college, but since they were basically a battle of who knows the most facts, and my hobby was reading the encyclopedia, I quickly moved up grades until I landed on the senior team. I was playing against eighteen-year-olds and just dominating them. I don't curse much, but I'm going to say it: THEY WERE MY BITCHES. It's not really anything to brag about, because it's pretty nerdy, but it was a big deal to me at the time. And I only got better and better until I became a legend—a little legend in my little town, but a legend nonetheless. I was basically the Uncle Rico of Quiz Bowl. Still living the dream, years later.

Being a Quiz Bowl god went to my head, too; I thought I knew *everything*. My hand was glued to that buzzer. So when a question came up that I didn't know the answer to, I still hit the buzzer. I remember the question to this very day: "What's the national holiday for trees?" Well, I know the answer now—Arbor Day—but at the time I buzzed in, I didn't have a clue. This was smack in the middle of a big tournament with a huge rival. *Oh crap.*

"I don't know," I said, "but I bet it's tree-mendous!"

My line got a big laugh—and me kicked off the team for the next couple of games. It was funny for a second but then not funny at all. I hated having to sit out even one round. I wanted to compete in a match, all the time. It wasn't so much that I loved winning as that I hated losing. I felt like people were looking down on me when I lost, and I didn't want to give them any more reasons to look down on me than they already had. See, it was never about being superior. I just didn't want to be inferior.

I really was a huge nerd. I mean, for starters, there were my glasses. I've had terrible eyesight from as early as I can remember. I'm color-blind and my right eye has never worked. I was born with a severe astigmatism, which could have been fixed if the intervention had been done early enough. So at five years old, I was given a patch to wear and became the pirate who got beaten up on the bus to kindergarten. Imagine being the poor kid *and* the pirate. I mean, if you're rich and a pirate, that's kind of awesome. But the poor dirty kid who was the pirate, that's begging to get annihilated.

Each time I wore the patch, they would beat the crap out of me, break my glasses, and throw my patch out the window. By the third time, I told my mom, "You can send me to school with the patch, but I'll take it off as soon as you can't see me."

True to my word, I stopped wearing the patch (and my glasses for years) and my eyesight in my right eye grew worse and worse until it got to the point where it is today. I can't see shape or color at all with my right eye, only light and darkness. For a while I asked about new medical techniques whenever they came out, but they were never for my eye because the real problem, the experts explained, is in my brain. Come to think of it, many experts have explained to me that I have a lot of problems in my brain, not just my eyesight. But the short of it is, my right eye doesn't work.

When I entered junior high school, not only did I have bad eyesight and need to wear glasses, I was also very small. Minuscule. I didn't grow much until my senior year, and didn't really get to my full height until college. To make matters worse, the school in Mountain Pine was split into two parts—kindergarten through sixth grade in a building at the bottom of a hill, and seventh through twelfth grade a hundred yards up the hill. So as a seventh grader, already small for my age, I had the pleasure of going to a school with twelfth graders who looked like giants.

I was an easy and obvious target. Being one of the poorer kids didn't help. Although my goal was not to wear the same clothes two days in a row (certain suicide), that wasn't easy because I didn't have a lot of clothes to wear. I certainly didn't have "outfits." I do love a good outfit now, though. Having a little money does allow me that luxury known as "outfits." I came up with an elaborate mix-and-match scheme that had the same clothes appearing every three days in different ways so as not to attract attention. I'd turn stuff inside out. Wear it backward and say, "Yeah, Kris Kross, you know." For those readers who don't know Kris Kross, take a second and educate yourself in legit kid rappers. Dang. Everyone wanted to be like Kris Kross back in the day. Once I wore one of my few pairs of pants to school backward (like the aforementioned Kris Kross) and broke the button off the front. I thought my mom was going to kill me. "You aren't a rapper," she said. Little did she know, years later I'd sign a recording contract as a rapper named Captain Caucasian. No joke.

Despite my best efforts, embarrassing things always seemed to happen to me. We all have a humiliating moment from childhood, the one where if someone asks you about your most embarrassing moment—bam!—it comes to mind immediately. For me, that moment came in eighth grade during the football off-season. Coach decided we should wrestle. The entire team sat around a mat that Coach Gandolph had thrown on the ground. "You, you—go!" he'd call out two guys at random, and you would have to get out in the middle and hit the mat.

I didn't want to wrestle anyone. I was the smallest guy on the team. But I couldn't *not* wrestle. So when Coach called me, I stood up in my loosely fitting blue spandex wrestling shorts and threw all ninety pounds of me into the match. At a certain point, while I was working hard at a takedown but not getting anywhere, I noticed that everyone was laughing and pointing at me. I'll be honest, people laughed and pointed at me a lot, so I didn't think much of it. But when the guy I was wrestling started to back away, and not out of fear of my mean moves, I knew something was up.

Unable to figure out what was going on, I looked around and then noticed where the boys were pointing. I looked down and saw a hole had ripped in my shorts. But that wasn't the worst part. The worst part was what was sticking out of the hole.

After that everything became a blur. I was so humiliated, I stumbled back to the edge of the mat and covered myself while everyone laughed harder and harder. Even Coach laughed. I don't think they had another wrestling match that day.

Now, if anything so much as touches the shoulder of a thirteen-year-old boy, it's going to elicit a physical reaction. It's just a fact of life. At that age, your body is doing all kinds of crazy things that it has no control over. Apparently, though, my boner made a huge impression on my peers, because they started calling me T-Bone. But getting an erection wrestling another guy in a small town in Arkansas is not really what you want to be known for.

The next day *everyone* was calling me T-Bone. When I walked into class or the cafeteria, they began chanting, "T-Bone, T-Bone, T-Bone, T-Bone!" I went into the bathroom and cried. It was awful and it didn't go away. A name like that really sticks. Kids calling me T-Bone became a daily thing. I hated it so much, I stopped going to any school events that weren't football games or Quiz Bowl.

Eventually the loud chanting wherever I went subsided, but the name never left me. There are guys I see now when I'm back home who still call me T-Bone—and it still sucks. Even in your thirties, being called a stupid nickname from eighth grade can make you feel crappy. Luckily, by the time I was a junior in high school, I finally got to a place where I didn't want to jump off a bridge every time someone called me that.

So if you're reading this and you're a kid, Holy cow! It gets better. (Although I don't know if you should be reading this if you're a kid . . .) This book process is weird. As I wrote the story about "T-Bone" the first time, I didn't think much about it. But reading it back during the editing phase, I literally said out loud, "OHHH, NOOOO." It almost felt as if I didn't know the story. The truth is that I cried more about the T-Bone incident than I wrote above in the story. I cried every day after school for probably close to three years. I don't know why I held back. And I also didn't mean it when I said "it gets better." It gets *way* better. And it gets as good as you make it. You can change how you feel about yourself. And the better you feel about yourself, and the better you treat others, the better you get treated. Yeah, it's a cliché, but clichés exist for a reason. So I'm going to write the following lines in a therapeutic way: I, Bobby Estell, am glad I got a public boner in eighth grade. It made me who I am today. Okay, that felt good. Back to the story.

Everyone got bullied where I went to school, except for the bullies, of course. There were three or four awful kids who tormented me. If they weren't calling me names, they were shoving me in the hallways. The worst one of the group, King Mean Guy #1, hounded me the entire six years we were in school together. He was bigger than I was, not only because he developed early but also because he had been held back a grade, so he was older. Which meant he was dumber, too. He loved to make me call him King Mean Guy #1.

He gave me quick daily doses of bullying: knocking my books onto the floor of the hallway in between classes, punching me in my shoulder over and over until I admitted he was the king, spitting in my food. But the worst incident, by far, was in the cafeteria during ninth grade. I was just sitting at a table by myself, eating lunch alone like I did every day, and still do today, *by choice,* when King Mean Guy #1 came up to me out of the blue and said, "Hey, you're in my seat."

"These aren't assigned seats," I said. I might have been small, but I had a big mouth. I could never beat King Mean Guy #1 physically, but mentally there was no contest.

"If you don't get out of my seat I'm going to make you get out of my seat."

"I'm going to sit *here.*"

I had been beaten up so many times before. What was one

more? But King Mean Guy #1 was a bully, and those guys trade in attention and power. Him pushing me out of his seat would have been boring, and at this point everyone in the cafeteria was looking in our direction to see what was happening. I was being challenged, and the pressure was on.

But instead of pummeling me, he unscrewed the cap to the ketchup bottle on the table and dumped it all on my head.

I didn't do anything. I didn't react or get up or try to wipe any of the ketchup dripping down my head and into my eyes and ears. I just sat there and continued to eat. The ultimate act of defiance against a bully is to ignore him. King Mean Guy #1 pushed me and then grabbed another bottle of ketchup from the table behind him and dumped that one all over my head, too.

Now I had *two* bottles of ketchup all over my head, my face, and my clothes. At this point I remained glued in my seat not out of defiance but sheer humiliation. I was too embarrassed to get up out of my chair and go to the bathroom to clean up. So I sat there and finished lunch, covered in ketchup. With everyone laughing at me.

When I was done, I finally got up, put my tray away like I did whenever I ate lunch, and left the cafeteria and the school entirely. Then I walked the mile and a half home, covered in ketchup.

Normally when I got bullied, I was okay with it because on a deep level I had the confidence that one day those guys were going to regret beating the crap out of me at school. I was smart and would be so successful, they would rue the day they picked on Bobby Estell. I had to feel that way to survive. If I hadn't, I would never have gotten out of Mountain Pine. So, generally, I protected myself with the old one-day-you'll-see thing. But this was the one moment in my life where I wish I had stood up for myself. I was a coward just to sit there drenched in ketchup. It still bothers me. Worse than the boner.

I hated being complicit in showing my own weakness. I couldn't let it go. I had such a chip on my shoulder about the fact that I had so many deficits. Everywhere I looked I saw kids with things I didn't have, things they took for granted, things like dads, rules, and braces. Braces weren't anything to be jealous of, but they made me mad, because I had crooked teeth with who knows how many cavities.

That chip came with me wherever I went, even on the vacation with Evan's family that I mentioned earlier. As I was packing, during the summer after ninth grade, I had that mix of excitement and dread that followed me around so much of the time. I had never been on vacation before, and it would also be my first time out of Arkansas. We were driving in a van to Colorado. I couldn't wait to get out of my stepdad's cramped but still-awesome-to-have house and go to Colorado—Colorado! But at the same time I worried about the trip. How did people act on a family vacation? Especially when the family wasn't theirs.

We drove up mountains the likes of which I'd never seen before and rode horses. I remember all parts of the trip so vividly, even sitting in the hotel room watching the world premiere of Michael Jackson's "You Are Not Alone" video. Why do I remember that? Because I was in a freaking hotel! I never got to do that. And I was watching MTV! We didn't have MTV. It was amazing.

The McGrews were as generous with me as anyone could be. They took me on vacation like I was their son and even bought me a T-shirt with COLORADO printed across it. I loved that shirt.

And yet I still harbored resentment toward them (even as I fought the feeling), just as I resented everyone who had more than me. Evan's family was by no stretch of the imagination rich. His mom was a schoolteacher and his dad was a freaking war hero drawing disability. But in my book, if you owned a van and drove it to Colorado to ride horses, you had money. I never showed my resentment in any way. Instead I kept it all inside, but I thought Evan had it so much easier than me and I held that against him. I hate myself now for feeling this way. These were the greatest, most loving humans in my life. I know that my bitterness stemmed from a deep insecurity. When we got home from Colorado, I begged Jerry McGrew to let me rake his leaves, cut his grass, anything to even the field.

Without money, size, or straight teeth, I had to come up with some sort of defense mechanism to guard myself against complete self-esteem annihilation—which is why I cracked jokes. I became an oddly introverted extrovert, which is what I am to this day. I was very alone and quiet and guarded most of the time. And then when I had an occasion to be on, I was really on. I didn't talk a lot, but when I did, I insisted everyone watch or listen to everything I did or said. I would sit at home and write "jokes." I memorized funny movie lines and practiced in my best voice, which I guess was practice to become a radio announcer. I spent countless hours alone at home practicing for the three minutes people would pay attention to me. (It's not unlike my life now, where I'm alone in my room for hours on end, practicing for the few hours a day people somewhat care what I have to say.)

The idea that you could use your flaws to your benefit and that a quirky guy could be a star was obviously appealing to me. That's part of the reason why my hero growing up was David

Letterman. I used to get up when I was eight years old and switch the channel to NBC while my mom slept in her chair so I could watch *Late Night*. I didn't know what the jokes meant, but I was still fascinated. No explanation was needed for the crazy physical stunts he did—like throwing watermelons off buildings and jumping into Styrofoam Dumpsters. That was hysterical and like nothing I'd ever seen before on TV. After I learned a little more about his life, I liked Letterman even more. I couldn't believe that he had started out as a weatherman. Even during that job, though, he didn't seem to have taken things too seriously (I read that he would sometimes report the weather of made-up cities, which got him into trouble). I admired the fact that he took a lot of risks and failed a lot—including a morning TV show that was canceled after only a couple of months. For obvious reasons I related to underdogs. He was even goofy looking like me. While watching Letterman and his dry, silly delivery night after night, I thought, I want to be like this person.

In the meantime, though, I had to survive high school. I loved to get a laugh more than anything, but sometimes I directed my humor at the wrong folks. Once, during my freshman year, I overheard two seniors, huge linemen on the varsity football team who could have easily been mistaken for middle-aged mill workers, complaining about the game they lost. Our JV team had won our latest game and I just couldn't help myself.

"So you guys lost?" I said. "Again? That must sting. We won. Again. Let me know if you want JV to show you a few moves."

Missing my clearly brilliant humor, the mill workers escorted me directly to the bathroom, picked me up, and shoved me into a stall, where I came face-to-face with the toilet. I couldn't avoid the high-school-style waterboarding coming my way, but I fought it just long enough to flush the toilet. Then they dunked my whole head and held me down while they flushed again. As the water rushed around my head, I thought, Well, I was going in anyway. Now at least it's clean water. And then for a second I thought I was going to drown in the toilet: This is how I'm going to die. (Spoiler alert: I didn't die.)

After the seniors released me, I went back about my business and headed to class—even though I had a soaking wet head. One thing you can say about me, I don't give up easily.

3

SMOOTH OPERATOR

People ask me all the time how I got into radio, and I'm always happy to tell the story because it's a testament to the fact that to make it, you don't have to know someone in the biz; have a friend that knows someone in the biz; or have a cousin whose mailman's uncle knows someone in the biz and owes your cousin a favor. All I knew was what I wanted to do, which was be on the air. And I was going to take any job that would lead me to getting to that spot.

I didn't have any connections to radio, only passion. I had decided that radio was my calling after my fifth birthday, when my aunt Cindy bought me a small radio. But that wasn't the only present. She had the local station's DJ say, "Happy Birthday to Bobby Estell," which we listened to on my little radio. And from that moment on I knew that *I* was going to be that DJ on the radio. When my kindergarten teacher had us fill out a paper that asked, "What do you want to be when you grow up?" I answered, "I want to be on the radio and TV, and I want to be a stand-up comedian." If I were handed the same piece of paper right now, I'd answer the same exact way. Almost thirty years later. How crazy is that?

The moment the DJ wished me a happy birthday I also became obsessed with our local Top 40 radio station, 105.9 KLAZ. When I got a little older, I called in to the station almost every night. So when I was twelve years old and I won a contest where you got to guest DJ for the night, it was as if I had won Powerball.

At this point I had been calling the station every night for years, begging to be put on the air. I even had created a DJ name for myself, Bobby the Barbarian, in a really dumb homage to one of my favorite professional wrestlers who went by the moniker "The Barbarian." Sting was my all-time favorite, but Bobby the Stinger didn't have the right ring. It would be cool if Sting read this book. Actually, when I think about it, here in descending order are the top five people that I remember from my childhood who I'd love to read this book:

5. Sting: The blond wrestling Sting. Not the Kristen Stewart Goth Sting.
4. Alyssa Milano: My childhood crush. I loved *Who's the Boss?* Mostly because of her.
3. Mark Grace: The former Cubs first baseman was my favorite baseball player growing up.
2. Kate Beckinsale: My lifelong crush. I'd drink all of her bathtub water. But not in a creepy way (in case you are reading this, Kate).
1. The entire cast of *Home Improvement*.

Back to my childhood obsession with the local radio station. Occasionally, Flyin' Brian, the guy who worked nights, would let me on the air to introduce a song.

"Hey, everybody," I would say on air. "It's Bobby the Barbarian. And at number three in the countdown it's Divinyls with 'I Touch Myself'—on KLAZ." I had no idea what that song title meant, although I became all too familiar with its meaning over the next . . . twenty years.

As soon as the station publicized the contest in which you had to write a poem for a shot at guest DJ'ing for a night, I poured my heart into a series of verses.

"Hey, everybody, there, up at KLAZ," my poem began, "Bobby the Barbarian, yo, that's me."

Kendrick Lamar, watch out. (For the record, I was just going to write "Kendrick, watch out," but even though I think I have the street cred to call him Kendrick—even if no one else does—I felt it more appropriate to use his full name, at least in a book. I also thought about going with 2Pac in that reference, but then realized that the much younger audience that is surely reading this book would have no idea about the cultural significance of 2Pac.)

Even though I didn't have the lyrical stylings of a 2Pac or Biggie Smalls (another ancient rap reference, for those counting at home), for some reason, the powers that be at KLAZ chose me as the winner. Maybe they felt sorry for Bobby the Barbarian or maybe this was their way to get me to stop calling every night. Either way, on Christmas Eve, I got the best present I could imagine: a shot as guest DJ.

The moment I walked into the studio it was love at first sight. A love that quick has only happened three times in my life: with a radio studio, my dog, and Kate Beckinsale (more on her later). The studio seemed massive and awesome. (It was actually tiny and quite crappy.) Surrounded by all these buttons, shiny lights, and microphones, I pictured millions of people listening as I began, "Hey y'all, it's Bobby the Barbarian . . ." (In reality, fifty people tops were listening. I mean, it *was* Christmas Eve.)

The moment was surreal because here I was on the other side of the radio, which was my favorite thing in life. Because I grew up sleeping on the couch with people walking by or the TV playing, that kind of constant noise became comfortable. If nothing was happening, I couldn't fall asleep. (I still don't sleep well if it's dark and quiet. My heart beats fast and I get really anxious. I sleep better on a couch with ten people in the room than alone in silence. So if I turn on the TV or the radio, it puts me back in my comfort zone.)

When my mom was out, and there was no noise to keep me company when I went to bed, I listened to the radio. I liked music of all kinds—still do. Living in Arkansas, there was obviously a heavy country music influence. But I was also into nineties grunge and alternative and hip-hop (see above 2Pac and Biggie references). I didn't see any problem jumping from Garth Brooks to Nirvana to Cypress Hill. Good music is good music.

But I didn't call KLAZ every night because of the music. I wanted to be in radio because I wanted to talk. I wanted people to hear my opinions. I wanted to entertain.

I had my favorite radio personalities, one of whom was the Outlaw Tommy Smith. He's still on in Little Rock, where I listened to him every morning. He and his sidekick, Big Dave Sanders, were pretty outlandish for the time and place. When they talked about booze and butts, which they did a lot, I said to myself, "This is crazy! I can't believe they're doing this on the air!" In reality, their morning show was a Howard Stern copycat. I had no idea, because I didn't know who Howard Stern was and wouldn't learn of Stern, who truly is the King of All Media, until I saw his movie *Private Parts* in college. But I looked up to Tommy Smith like crazy for the longest time.

As I prepared to graduate from high school in the spring of 1998, I was still a starry-eyed kid who had one goal and one goal only: to work for KLAZ. With the naive confidence that only eighteen-year-olds have, I got myself an interview with Kevin Cruise, the program director and afternoon host of KLAZ, through sheer persistence. I basically went into the same radio station where I had guest DJ'ed on Christmas Eve six years earlier and begged for a job. Sitting across the desk from Kevin, a small guy with a thin mustache, I offered up my only qualifications (other than that I was willing to work for no pay): "I'll do whatever you'll let me do, and I'll be on time."

"I'll think about it," he said.

Unbelievably, Kevin called me a few days later to say yes. I wasn't hired to be the new morning-show personality or anything, just to clean the lobby on Sundays and switch out a Rick Dees Top 40 countdown. (Back in the days when the countdown was played on CD, you played half the countdown on one CD, switched it out, and then played the other half of the countdown on another. Super technologically advanced.) I think eventually I made five bucks an hour, but I would have seriously done it for free. I felt like the luckiest guy in the world.

As soon as I found out that I had a job working at KLAZ on Sundays, I called my high school guidance counselor to change where I was going to college from the University of Arkansas to

Henderson State University. Now, the fact that I was going to college at all was a major victory. Only a handful of kids from my high school went on to college—and no one in my family had ever been.

My senior year had been all about that goal. I was smart enough to know it wasn't enough to be smart. I also had to be good at the standardized admissions tests for college. There was a formula, and I needed that formula. So I spent my own money on an ACT prep course. I had saved up from my job at the marina on Lake Ouachita, where I pumped gas for boats and sold live bait to fishermen, like crickets and worms. The three-day class where I learned to take the test was worth every penny. My scores were good enough that I would be able to attend a state school on full scholarship. I wanted to go to the U of A. It had been my lifelong dream because of its football team, the Razorbacks. It was the team I loved so much that I physically hurt when they lost—and still do—so that's where I was going to college. That is, until I landed a job at KLAZ. It would have been impossible to work there in any meaningful way and attend U of A in Fayetteville, which was more than three hours away. So at the last minute, I had my guidance counselor, who used to work at Henderson State, pull some strings and transfer me to the four-year liberal arts college in Arkadelphia, only an hour away from Hot Springs.

It was a decision I made all on my own. My mom and my grandma, who never asked me if I was going to college in the first place, didn't know I switched to Henderson until I told them. I'm not even sure they knew I'd been planning to go to Arkansas, either. It didn't matter. I had a plan, and breaking into the radio business was more important than whatever university I attended.

My decision turned out to be even more important because a few days before what was supposed to be my first day at work, I got a call from Kevin. As it turned out, the station had had to fire the weekend DJs. I don't know the story behind it—I was just a kid—but the upshot was that Kevin needed someone to put on the air, and he needed someone immediately.

"We need *you* to go on the air," he said.

Me? I was hired to sweep up cigarette butts and switch a CD, not be on the air. I was a kid! Although I was scared to death, I said, "Great!"

"Okay, you need a name," he said. Everyone on radio had a cool name. "What do you want it to be, Bobby Z or Bobby Bones? You can pick either one of the two."

Now, I have no clue how or when he came up with those particular options, but I thought they were both terrible. Out of my two choices, at least Bobby Bones sounded like a real human. I mean, a pirate or a porn star—but still, a human. So I went with Bobby Bones. (I have never been able to shake that name, and although it's now just who I am, I still hate it. It's so stupid. For someone who built his career and identity on being authentic, having such a fake name has always bothered me. Not to mention the unfortunate echo of T-Bone, that nickname that haunted me as a kid. Although one had nothing to do with the other, a story quickly went around my hometown that I named myself *because of* the T-Bone story. As if I would give myself a nickname based on one of the worst moments in my life?)

"Congratulations," Kevin Cruise said after I picked my name. Then he tossed me an oversized white KLAZ T-shirt. I was probably a small, but the shirt was an XL. (Isn't it annoying that all free shirts seem to be XL? You're so excited to get it, and then you can't even wear it unless you want to look like you're going to sleep in your dad's T-shirt. I've seen many people get into fist-fights over shirts shot out of a T-shirt cannon, and I always want to shout, "It's not worth it! The shirt's the size of a circus tent!")

The night after I got my gigantic free T-shirt was Saturday and my first on-air. I'm only slightly exaggerating when I say it was the worst night of radio since the invention of the medium. I had no idea what I was doing, so I did most everything wrong. I pushed the wrong buttons; I announced the wrong station; I even played songs on top of each other. If it could go wrong, it did go wrong. But I got through it, and little Bobby Bones was born.

Although I was terrible, I loved every minute—being on air was a rush—and I wasn't so terrible that Kevin changed his mind about my doing Saturday and Sunday nights. I don't think he expected me to be good. He needed someone quickly, and I was the closest warm body. It was timing and the fact that I seemed trustworthy. Otherwise I showed no other promise that I can think of. I didn't even have a good voice. As I started my weekends on KLAZ (and for years after), I tried to be the guy with the deep broadcaster voice. You know, the voice of God. But I couldn't pull it off. I don't have a distinct voice, which now I recognize as a plus, because I sound like the regular guy I am.

I wanted to do a good job, because in my book this was the coolest job in the world. My first-ever radio interview was with Darius Rucker. You'll know him as either the lead singer of Hootie and the Blowfish or a country superstar—or maybe both—but I know him as one of the nicest guys I've ever been around. I was just some teenager from Nowhere, Arkansas, sent to an amphitheater in Little Rock to get an interview from one of my favorite bands. Petrified, I waited in a back room for one of the band members to come out, since the manager didn't specify which one he was sending out. No offense to Mark, Dean, or Sony (as a Blowfish fan I knew all of them), but I wanted Darius. And in he walked: Darius freaking Rucker. Naturally my response was to start shaking so badly, I couldn't hold the microphone steady. Darius took the mic from my quivering hand and led me though every single question. When we—or he—was done, he actually hugged me and said, "Keep up the good work."

Over the next couple months of doing weekends, my radio and interviewing skills improved (I wasn't playing two songs at the same time or shaking like a leaf when I talked to a celebrity anymore). But they didn't improve so much that I deserved the promotion I soon got from Kevin. However, when the night guy announced he was moving to Little Rock, Kevin offered me his spot. And at eighteen, I got my own night show on radio! Again, it had nothing to do with talent. I was simply at the right place at the right time—and had proven that I was reliable (which I maintain is half of the formula for success in life).

I knew I was incredibly lucky to get that opportunity, but it also meant I was starting a full-time job just as I was starting college. I signed up for twenty hours of credits for the semester (about five hours more than required, just in case I failed any-thing) with the full knowledge that I had a job every weekday night an hour away from my college. My schedule was only one of the many new things I had to get used to. Although Hender-son was by no means a huge, cosmopolitan campus, it was so different than the tiny place I came from.

That was pointed out to me on my very first day of school by Courtney, the one real friend I made in college. (Courtney is a dude, by the way.) We were both in an oral communications course, which I walked into wearing my high school letter-man jacket. After class, Courtney, a hulking guy who had been recruited to play quarterback for the football team, took me aside and said, "Dude, we don't wear high school jackets anymore. We're in college."

Humiliated, I felt like I was right back in junior high with everyone laughing at me. I might as well have had a boner. I stopped wearing the letterman jacket right away, but the problem was that I only had one coat—and that was it. So I ended up going to class in the freezing cold wearing just a sweatshirt until I saved up enough to buy a new coat.

Although I was embarrassed when Courtney called me out for wearing high school apparel in college, I also appreciated him for it. He was a college quarterback and I was a nerd in Buddy Holly–style glasses. But appearances aside, we had a lot in common. Courtney was from Hope, Arkansas, which was the same kind of place as Mountain Pine. We were both broke and busting our butts to get through school. After meeting in that communications course, we started to hang out. He was supportive of my career, rooting me on as I struggled to keep my job and get my homework done. I asked him how practice was and gave him free CDs. We were in it together.

(Courtney is still my best friend; if I were to get married he would definitely be my best man. Mainly, that's because Court-ney is just a really good dude, and we've had a lot of good times together. But another reason is that he was my best friend when *nobody* wanted to be my friend. Now that I've achieved some success, I worry about motivations in almost every relationship. Why do people want to be my friends? Is it because I'm on the radio? Is it because I'm not poor anymore? I just have to trust that people like me for me, and it isn't easy. With Courtney there was never a question.)

The fact that Courtney was my only friend at Henderson was fine, because honestly, I really didn't have time for friends. Check out what was a typical day in the life of Bobby Estell's college career:

- ♪ wake up at 8 A.M. and go to class
- ♪ spend most of the day in class
- ♪ drive an hour to KLAZ to work from 4 P.M. to midnight
- ♪ get back in the car and drive three-quarters of the way back to college and stop at Waffle House, where I study until 3 A.M.
- ♪ get into bed at 4 A.M.
- ♪ wake up at 8 A.M. and do it all again

And that was just freshman year. Because my scholarship required work credits, I worked at and eventually ran the college radio station, KSWH 91.1 FM, too. I pretty much had every job at the station from radio host to program director to general manager.

I remember people telling me when I was at Henderson, "Wait until after college, that's when life gets really hard." Not for me. College was the grind. No matter how hard it got or how tired I was, I couldn't quit anything. While I was certain radio was going to be my career, it was also crucial to me that I get my degree. I was determined to be the first person in my family to graduate college. It was truly the first time in my life I had to "Fight. Grind. And repeat."

The result was that during college, I never had five minutes to myself. Every minute of every day was full of something—including spending afternoons trying to lose my accent. Right across the street from Henderson's campus was another college, Ouachita Baptist University, which offered a speech pathology major. And I definitely considered the accent I got from growing up in Mountain Pine a pathology. I mean it was reeeeeal thick. If I was going to have a successful career in radio and break out of my little neck of the woods, I had to scrub from my tongue the Dirty South (note: it's not dirty South; it's Dirty South! I still represent). That's what I attempted to do, several hours each week, at Ouachita Baptist, where I got free speech therapy from students training for a degree in this area. My *i*'s were "ahs" and *g*'s at the end of a word just didn't exist. "Fishing" was "fishin'." I spent years working on my damn *i*'s and *g*'s.

I wish I could say that my hectic schedule was the real reason that I wasn't exactly the most popular guy at Henderson. The truth is there was a much bigger impediment to me being the life of the frat parties (that I never attended): I had never touched a drop of alcohol and never intended to.

I don't remember ever making a conscious decision not to use drugs or alcohol. There was never that after-school-special moment where kids at a party were pressuring me to pound a beer, but I said to myself, I'm not drinking. No, my commitment to abstinence was always a part of my makeup. I have always known I would avoid drinking my whole life.

Clearly, my abstinence was a reaction to my mom. From early on, I saw the effect of alcohol not only on her but also on a lot of other adults around me. From that I took away a few lessons. When my mom came home drunk, I was scared—not for myself, never for myself, but for her. I never wanted to put others in that situation. If you have a certain genetic or psychological makeup like my mother, you can't control your alcohol intake. Any amount, no matter how little, is poison. And I suspected that if I tested it, I would find out that my mom and I were more alike than we were different.

Even in high school, when a lot of kids get into alcohol as a way to navigate the troubled waters of adolescent social life, I was never tempted. It should come as no surprise that as the kid with the nickname who had ketchup dumped on his head in the cafeteria, I did not get invited to a lot of parties. So that limited the amount of peer pressure I was exposed to. But even if I had gone to parties, I wouldn't have ever taken a beer. Peer pressure doesn't affect me. For me, pressure comes from within. Some guy shouting at me, "Drink! Drink! Drink!" is not pressure. That's just some idiot shouting. Pressure comes to me when I'm about to walk onto a stage where a crowd has paid good money to be entertained.

However, my choice not to drink made me an anomaly at Henderson. At college in the rural South, there isn't so much to do. So, there's generally a lot of time to drink and party. But for me it was never an option. To this day, I've never touched alcohol, an illegal drug, cigarettes. Nothing. I've never even tried coffee. I'm not morally against alcohol. No judgments at all. Matter of fact, if my friends aren't drinking, they're not fun. But I saw what my mom went through and can feel that demon inside of me.

Don't get me wrong. Despite my unwavering conviction, being a teetotaler wasn't easy. There was a part of me that was jealous when I watched people around me get drunk. I was envious at the way they could let loose and have fun. I knew I wouldn't be able to drink in any sort of moderation—that if I started it's all I would want to do, all the time. I didn't want alcohol to become a bigger influence on my life than it already was, and I knew that if I made drinking an issue (meaning not wanting to be around others while *they* drank), it would divide me from others.

It was (and is) my biggest fear that people would change their behavior on my account. I never wanted anyone to feel uncomfortable drinking around me, so one of my strategies was to fake-drink. I would order Coke or club soda with a lime in a small glass. There are many ways to make it look like you're drinking. I also made myself useful by being the designated driver.

I was also quite happy to hang out in bars on the weekend until the wee hours of the morning, as my friends got progressively more drunk and incoherent, for one reason and one reason only: I wanted to meet girls.

Spending countless hours at nightclubs (we'd show up to the Electric Cowboy in Little Rock at 11 P.M. and I'd dance until the sun came up), I did meet a lot of girls—it was just that none of them wanted to meet me. I was familiar with that situation from my high school days, as evidenced by my first kiss.

It was during the summer after my sophomore year of high school and I was working as a roofer in Kansas City, Missouri. My mom's brother, Don Hurt, got me the job. Uncle Bub (what we called him) had been in a lot of trouble in his life. He'd been in jail; he'd been all over. (An alcoholic, he was eventually found dead in his trailer. He was only in his forties.) I really liked Uncle Bub, but even more important, I had to make money for school clothes. So I went up to Kansas City for the summer to help him roof houses. My job required the least amount of skill. I did tear-offs (stick the shovel under the nails; use your foot to pry up the roof; tear off a piece; throw it down on the ground) and cleanups (cleaning up everything I'd thrown on the ground).

Uncle Bub had a friend on the crew with two daughters, one of whom was my age. One night, the sisters and a couple of other kids invited me to hang out with them. There were six of us, and someone suggested we play Spin the Bottle. I was nervous because I had never kissed a girl. Let me remind you, I was a sophomore in high school. There were kids in my class who already had babies, and I still hadn't made it to first base.

No one in the group gathered around the bottle knew I hadn't kissed a girl, but that didn't make me feel any better. The bottle spun around and landed on the sister my age, a blond sixteen-year-old who was already very developed. Then it spun again . . . and landed on me.

She was *not* a happy camper.

How do I know this? Because she was very vocal about her displeasure. "Oh, you've got to be kidding me!" she said. "I hate this game." As I write this, I just felt that disgusted feeling again. The same one I had when I wrote the T-Bone story just a few pages back. I am such a loser.

But she did it. I had to give her credit, she held true to the rules of the game. That was my first kiss—with someone who wanted to have nothing to do with me. So it shouldn't come as a surprise that it wasn't until I got to college that I finally got a girlfriend.

It took me the longest time to get the nerve up to ask out (fake name alert) Farah (with an *h*, always with an *h*, and if you didn't put an *h*, you'd have to hear about why the *h* was so important to her. And that's true. Just her name wasn't Farah. But it did end with an *h*). I could tell she was awesome as soon as I met her. The cousin of my roommate's girlfriend, she was smart, pretty, and together. I didn't think I had a chance with her.

I was scared of girls, especially pretty ones like Farah, because they never liked me. It's just like if a dog gets hit a bunch, he'll flinch whenever someone raises his hand. I had been rejected so much I was scared of putting myself out there. But somehow I got the nerve to ask Farah out. I remember the smooth pickup line I used the first time I asked if she wanted to hang out: "Hey, ummm, can we eat sometime?" Feel free to use that whenever you need, and don't say I never gave you anything.

Farah was awesome. She was smart. She challenged me on my beliefs. She had parents who were still together and loved each other. I enjoyed everything about her. Well, almost everything. She and I dated for a long time before we had sex—like, a long time. Unlike the stereotypical scenario where the girl is the one who refuses to put out, in this case I was the one who wouldn't do it. I was scared to death.

I was always scared of sex. Different than my fear of rejection from women, this stemmed from my mom getting pregnant with me when she was fifteen. I never wanted to have a kid and certainly didn't have the money to support one. Because of that early and indelible imprint on my personality, I have never been the type to go out and try to get lucky. I've only ever had sex with real girlfriends. And myself. Lots of that. I can't get me pregnant!

BEFORE I DID THE DEED WITH FARAH, I WANTED TO DO MY homework. Because I was already in my twenties and still completely inexperienced, I didn't want to be, as my grandma would say, "like a cub bear playing with his peter." In my quest to learn what made women feel good, I turned to the best source of sex education: the Internet. Now, I'm not talking about porn. I'm not a porn guy. Never have been. Not for any moralistic reason, I'm just not into it. No, I did some bona fide research on how to have sex and more specifically what women like while having sex.

On the big night, I implemented some of my learning and was, as they say, going down on Farah when all of a sudden, I tasted blood. That brought things to an abrupt halt, as you might imagine.

"Bobby, your nose is bleeding!" she said.

For my entire life, I always got nosebleeds when I was in warm situations. I remember waking up as a kid with blood all over my pillow if it was too humid. But to have a nosebleed during my first sexual act when already I had no idea what I was doing? I was so embarrassed. I had thought it was her. But it wasn't; it was *me*.

I have had no shortage of mortifying experiences in my life, but this was hands-down the worst, even worse than the wrestling boner. I was every word for embarrassed that you can think of. I mean, even writing about it now makes me feel sorry for me. I was so embarrassed that I could have easily left and never talked to Farah again. Luckily for me, Farah was way more mature and refused to let that be our last moment together. Still, I couldn't fool around with her for a long time for fear that I'd mess it up again. Eventually, somehow she convinced me to relax, and at the age of twenty-two (you read that right!) I finally lost my virginity. I could make some joke about it "being the best six seconds of her life," but that would be too easy. And probably not much of a joke at all.

Farah and I didn't last. (But why? you're thinking. You were such a stud!) The truth is that I didn't want to commit, which, as you will read, is the story of my life. She went on to become the successful professional and incredible mom I knew she would. And me? Well . . . I'm still single.

I wish I could say that I got better with more experience when it came to women, but my next girlfriend inspired another lackluster performance on my part. Samantha (fake name alert #2), a teacher who was a few years older than me, lived in the same apartment complex that I did my senior year of college. A tall brunette with an athletic build, she came from an affluent family and had graduated from one of the rich-kid high schools near mine. She was really pretty and had money—all of it was way too good for me. Samantha was completely out of my league, but I wore her down over months and months and months and months.

Farah did improve my confidence, in that I learned that if I could just get a girl to pay attention to me, I could get her to like me. The trick is getting them to pay attention, because when I walk into a bar, girls aren't bowled over by my good looks. The only thing that I have is a combination of wit and self-deprecating charm.

So after months of badgering her with my amazing wit, Samantha finally agreed to go out with me and eventually became Bobby Estell's second official girlfriend. But after dating for a while, she wound up moving back to her hometown, which was an hour and fifteen minutes away. Now, when you're a twenty-two-year-old college student, an hour and fifteen minutes might as well be South Korea.

There didn't seem any other answer than to break up, which we did. But after a few weeks of being apart, I decided I had made a mistake. I wanted Samantha back and knew exactly how to do it: the grand romantic gesture. I didn't have money for jewelry (heck, I barely had money for gas), so I did the next best thing and wrote her a song. Although I can't remember the words now, I spent a good few hours on the song, which I called "Let's Get Back Together." Subtle.

I put my guitar in the car and took off for her house on a Thursday, thinking that if she took me back we'd go out on Friday night. When I got into her driveway, I was excited to perform my love song. I knocked on her door, my guitar in one hand and a rose in the other. Perfect.

Samantha, who had no idea it was me outside, opened the door. And when she did I was the one taken off guard, because there was a dude on her couch—a big dude.

Before he could see me standing there with a rose and guitar and decide to come out and beat me up—which he or anyone else could have easily done (you don't have to be big, or a dude; I'm pretty easy to beat up)—Samantha shut the door behind her and walked out onto the porch.

"What are you doing?" she whispered.

What was I doing? I know what any self-respecting guy would have done—packed up his stuff and gone home. But not me. Instead, I insisted on going through with my plan, even if it had become a suicide mission.

"I wrote you this song," I said, handing her the rose. "I'd like to sing it for you."

I strummed the guitar and performed "Let's Get Back Together," maybe because I like the pain. Or maybe because I wrote this song, had driven an hour and fifteen minutes, and that was the plan. I can't remember a single line of that terrible tune;

I've blocked it out. But when I was done, Samantha said, "Uh, thanks. You need to go now."

Then she gave me the rose back and closed the door.

Walking back to my car, I saw her new boyfriend's monster truck parked on the left side of her house. How had I missed that before? I guess I was blinded by the fact that I was about to play this love song, which was going to sweep Samantha off her feet, and then we were going to be back together and go on a romantic date the next night! That's all I was thinking about.

I learned an important lesson that night. If you ever knock on an ex's door and there's another guy sitting on the couch inside, just pack it up and go home.

COUNTRY MOUSE
IN THE BIG CITY

Driving across the Broadway Bridge, which led into downtown Little Rock, I was overwhelmed by the sight of skyscrapers—well, tall buildings, anyway—that rose up behind the arches of the bridge. The state capitol was here! I'm from Mountain Pine, where 700 people live. The nearest city, Hot Springs, was a town of 30,000. Little Rock had a population of nearly 190,000. The city across the Arkansas River felt like the biggest one in the world.

I couldn't believe I was going to live in this place with guys in suits and briefcases rushing around, fancy shopping malls, and restaurants with all kinds of food like Greek and even Japanese. One of the first things I did when I moved there was go to one of those restaurants where they cook the food on the grill in front of you. And when that dude flipped the shrimp tail in his pocket, I wanted to give him a standing ovation! They even had TV news stations in Little Rock. I drove by the studios of KATV, where chief meteorologist Ned Perme reported on the weather. When I was a kid my grandma never missed his weather report. I was starstruck just thinking about it; I was working in the same city as Ned Perme!

Working in Little Rock had been a dream of mine ever since I was a kid, and my stepdad took me down to the city for a Travelers baseball game, which we did maybe once a year. Thing was, I was never too clear on how I was going to actually get to Little Rock. That was many railroad tracks away from Mountain Pine. But shortly before graduating from Henderson in 2002, I forced my way into the offices of Q-100, Little Rock's Top 40 station, and just like I had done with KLAZ, begged for a job. Now, I wish I could say that it was my sharp wit or the impressive reputation I had gained doing nights for the last four years in Hot Springs that convinced the program director at Q-100 to give me a job. But I think what clinched it was the fact that I took less money than I was currently making at KLAZ—and I was making none to begin with. It didn't matter to me. When I signed my contract for seventeen thousand dollars a year to do nights for Q-100, I was the happiest guy in the world.

I didn't even mind that it meant my commute to and from college, which I still had to finish up, was longer—although I was ready to be done with the grind that was my college experience. I felt that school was holding me back from my life and my career. But I understood it was important for me to finish my education. If I failed in radio, I would always have that degree.

Even more motivating than securing an insurance policy for myself by graduating from college was setting an example for my sister and other people from my hometown that anyone could do it. I still have the same drive to show people that anything can be achieved, no matter how big it is, if you set your mind to it. I've really forced my way into accomplishing things—not out of talent but out of hard work and just refusing to stop. What I believe and say so often (ad nauseam, if you listen to my show, maybe even in this book; I'll check) is that being on time and not giving up are the two most important elements of success. At least they were to me. They were two things that I could control, and I worked them as hard as I could.

Even during the most difficult days of college—when I was juggling exams and extra shifts at the radio station—I never felt like I was going to crack. It wasn't an option. The lack of any kind of safety net only served to push me to greater extremes. I took way too many classes every semester not because of my passion for learning but because I felt like I needed to in order to stay ahead of things. What if I got sick or I got in a car wreck and couldn't go to school for a semester? I couldn't afford to lose any time. So I hoarded credits just in case something bad happened to me. It was a real disaster mentality, to be sure, but one that helped me to graduate early. The weird thing about me is that I still use this mentality in different elements of my life. I'm the kind of person who wants to overpay my bills by a few dollars every month. And for the same reasons. What if I get fired and don't have a job? I need a cushion to be able to survive "just in case."

As soon as I had that degree in hand, I was out of Arkadelphia and on the highway to Little Rock, where I moved into a tiny two-bedroom apartment with a college buddy, Josh, and his wife. It was a good arrangement for all of us as we were just scraping by. Living with a pair of newlyweds didn't bother me in the least; I still considered having my own room a luxury since it was still so new to me. (Sad. I know.)

The first time I had my own bedroom still remains one of the highlights of my life. It was sophomore year of college, and Courtney and I had decided to share a two-bedroom apartment with rooms across the hall from each other. We paid our deposit, signed the lease to rent the place, and got the key. As soon as I walked in, I went straight up to the bedroom, shut the door, and sat on the floor of my room, *my room*. There was no furniture, but just the act of shutting the door was a revelation. Before then I never had a space I could call my own.

Other than bedrooms, Courtney and I shared everything that year—including a TV, a nineteen-inch Panasonic that we found at a yard sale because we couldn't afford a new one. This thing was no flat-screen; it was a beast. Still, we'd walk it back and forth to each other's room, dragging the cable wire behind. Luckily, Courtney and I had opposite schedules, so the TV share worked out.

Nothing that year could top the feeling I had when I first walked into my own room. Not a lot could top it in general. If I were to make a list of the greatest moments of my life, getting my own bedroom would be on it. (Maybe that's why now I never leave my bedroom. Minor emotional breakthrough! I have a nice place. I live downtown in Nashville, with plenty of space and a nice living room. I even have a pool table—obviously I'm still single as of the writing of this book! But I bet you I haven't watched TV in my living room more than ten times since I moved in over a year ago. I stay in my room. All the time. And I love it. It is still my happy space.)

When I first moved to Little Rock, I was happy to have a

cozy living situation with Josh and his wife. It was nice to have a few familiar faces around as I tried to find my way in the big city where there was so much for me to learn. In Little Rock you had to *pay* for parking. What in the world? It was an entirely new concept to me to take my hard-earned money and use it to park my car. This is what city folks did?

Of course, paying for parking was the least of it. The big city was also a huge lesson in crime. The kind of robberies I was used to growing up in Mountain Pine was someone stealing a handsaw or ice chest from someone's shed. Little Rock was a whole different story. As a whole, Arkansas has the dubious distinction of often ranking as one of the nation's most violent states (as well as one of the poorest). And within the state, Little Rock is one of the most violent cities. (In 2015, Little Rock earned the title of number one most dangerous city under two hundred thousand people in the United States, according to the FBI.)

I don't know if I got used to Little Rock's crime, but I sure got a taste of it one night while on my way to a radio station event at the Electric Cowboy, a mix between a megaclub and a country music bar. (There was a huge dance floor where they played country music for forty-five minutes and then Nelly for the next fifteen. And so forth for hours.)

I had brought along a girl who I was dating at the time (although looking back, I think she was dating like five dudes, and I was just a guy who got her into the Electric Cowboy for free.) Before we went into the event, I drove up to an ATM right on the side of the club. I had just slipped my bank card into the machine when I heard someone yell, "How much money you got in there, boy?"

I thought it was a joke, someone from the station or a listener pulling my leg. But when I turned around, what I saw wasn't funny at all. A man in a mask approached the driver's-side window and put a gun right up to my face. He dragged it from my cheekbone to my temple. And then he pressed. And pressed again, harder.

Now, as I've said in the past, I am no tough guy. Never have been. But in this empirically terrifying moment, I wasn't freaked out. Not because I had some sort of Clint Eastwood plan to wrestle the gun away from the dude but because the whole situation seemed fake. It was as if I were watching TV, not in the middle of a real-life situation.

Unfortunately, the guy in the mask was not an actor and the gun he put up to my head was not a prop. As he shoved the gun into my temple over and over, he yelled, "How much money you got in there?"

Not much. Actually, I was broke. I'm not exaggerating. I was making seventeen thousand dollars a year, which didn't leave a lot of cash after I paid rent, food, and gas. I probably had about thirty bucks or so in my bank account. In fact, I was only planning on taking out ten dollars so I had cash to buy my date a beer in case the club owner didn't hook me up. But the robber didn't care about my financial status.

"Whatever I have, I will give it all to you," I said calmly.

"Get it out, now," he said, pointing with his gun toward the ATM. And then he pistol-whipped me. He slammed the gun into my face with a down motion, stunning me. But oddly, it didn't hurt. I was running on pure adrenaline at that point.

There was only one problem with the plan: I completely blanked on my PIN number. In my defense, it's hard to think when there's a gun in your face.

"I can't remember my PIN number."

"I should kill your mothereffing ass right now!"

With a beanie on his head and a dark cover over his face, his eyes were all that I saw—and they were vividly staring at me.

"Get the money out, boy," he seethed.

Believe me, we were on the same page. All I wanted to do was get that thirty bucks out, give it to him, and get that gun out of my face. But I couldn't remember my PIN number to save my life. So he did what guys who hold guns to other people's heads do: he didn't pull the trigger (too much paperwork) but instead slammed me in the head again.

Wow, I'm getting pistol-whipped, I thought to myself. It was so surreal, it was as if I were watching the scene from above, and at any minute I could have opened my eyes.

"If I knew my PIN number, I would give you every bit of money I had," I pleaded. "The last thing I want you to do is shoot me or hit me with your gun again."

While the masked man by my side was getting increasingly angry, my date chose that moment to shove her purse and the wallet I had handed to her earlier under her seat. I guess she thought since his attention was on me, she could save our credit cards, driver's licenses, and . . . her makeup? It was a pretty stupid move, because just then we were both startled by a knocking on *her* window. There was another guy with a mask on, tapping her window with his gun in a motion for her to roll it down. We had been so consumed with the first guy that we had totally missed his accomplice. She put down her window, and he took her purse and my wallet. Meanwhile the guy by my window is still holding a gun to my head, repeating, "I'm going to effing kill you; I'm going to effing kill you."

It was looking pretty bad for Bobby Estell in that moment. I was about to die for thirty dollars, because I couldn't remember my stupid PIN number. (Incidentally, I never remembered it again. For the rest of my life, it was gone. Whatever part of my brain I stored that information in was erased.)

The dude then slammed me in the side of the head again with his gun, as hard as he could. That one, I felt a little bit.

"You're lucky I don't effing kill you," he said.

Then they took off running. He didn't kill me—or get my thirty dollars. If you're reading this now, Robber, what up? Guess who's got my thirty dollars? Me! (Well, I spent way over thirty dollars in therapy bills after that, because for a year straight I had nightmares every single night. Every single night it was the same scenario: the masked men robbing me at gunpoint, but this time I was in the actual bed where I was sleeping! It was terrifying. But at least the thug didn't get my thirty dollars, right?)

Okay, so I had just been pistol-whipped, robbed, and had my life threatened. You'd think the first thing I'd do would be to call the cops, right? No, not me. Being the guy always trying to turn a dime into a dollar, I called the TV news station instead. "I just got robbed at gunpoint," I told them.

My reasoning went like this: I knew the cops weren't going to catch those guys. They never catch those guys. To this day, they haven't caught those guys. Now that I wasn't dead from a gunshot to the head, I thought about it for a second: How can I get the most benefit from a bad situation? By calling the cops, having them come out only to *not* catch the thieves, and tell me *not* to call the news? Or, call the news first, have them do a story that might raise my profile a little and help me with ratings for my radio show, and *then* call the cops?

It was a no-brainer. I called the news, and three stations came out to the Electric Cowboy to cover it. Then I called the cops, who were pretty pissed that I decided to call the TV station before the police station.

I might have seemed pathetic to the Little Rock PD, but I had to get ratings to keep my job. I was still relatively new to Little Rock radio, and we had a main competitor in town that we were neck and neck with in terms of listener numbers. I couldn't afford to lose my 17K-a-year dream job. As much as I had loved working at Hobby Lobby as a teenager, I didn't want to go back.

I could write an entire chapter about my time at Hobby Lobby. I know that I've really only written about my radio career to this point, but I had many other jobs. I worked at the marina, did maintenance on a golf course, waited tables—and was an employee of Hobby Lobby. That position at Hobby Lobby was a big deal to me because I got to wear a vest. I remember my first day on the job, being given my blue vest, putting both arms through the armholes and puffing out my chest with pride. In the break room a few minutes before my first shift was about to start, all I had to do was get my name tag and I was ready to walk out onto the floor.

I went to the supervisor, who handed me my name tag, and thought to myself, How cool is this? I get to wear something on this already badass vest that tells people my name. It's almost like I'm famous. With name tag in hand, I went into the bathroom to pin it on. But as soon as I got in front of the bathroom mirror I went from totally psyched to completely bummed out. The reason? My name tag read, HOBBY LOBBY BOBBY.

How I didn't foresee that Hobby Lobby Bobby was going to be part of my Hobby Lobby experience I will never know.

But there I was (and to some remain to this day), Hobby Lobby Bobby. Even still, I loved working at Hobby Lobby. You can find ANYTHING for a crafts project. Need a picture frame? Check. A button in the shape of the Eiffel Tower? Check. Rainbow-colored pipe cleaner pack? Check!

Despite the cornucopia of craft supplies, I just didn't want my old job (or name tag) at Hobby Lobby back now that I was a DJ in Little Rock. Radio was my home. And I was going to do anything to keep it that way. Even using my second close call with death (yeah, there are even more besides falling on the boat trailer and being held up at gunpoint outside the Electric Cowboy) to my professional advantage.

In addition to using my own experience with violent assault as PR, I also worked hard on my night show to make it one listeners would want to tune in to. Naturally I played a bunch of music, but I also tried out anything and everything to see what worked on the radio. On air I played guitar, talked about current events, and interviewed the occasional pop star. I also kept trying to find what separated me from everyone else. And at the time, I hadn't really found it.

I was still trying to have a big voice, say things the "right" way, and time my talk breaks out perfectly. But I wasn't a natural. I remember streaming radio on the Internet and listening to guys like Kane at WFLZ in Tampa, Atom Smasher at KRBE in Houston, and Tony Fly at KDWB in Minneapolis and thinking, "I will never ever be as good as those guys." I knew I couldn't compete doing what they did. So I did the one thing that I could do better than anyone else. And that was be me. I talked on air about being single, being a dork, not knowing my dad—the list goes on and on. The more I divulged, the more real it felt. The more I divulged, the more comfortable I was being me—even if it was awkward driving through Taco Bell and having an employee say to me, "Sorry you got dumped last night." The oddness of strangers knowing every intimate detail of my life didn't take away from my sense of completion. It's totally counterintuitive, but from behind a microphone I felt safe talking about the most personal subjects, those things that I didn't feel comfortable talking about anywhere else.

My radio style took a long time to develop. Heck, I'm still developing, but it was in Little Rock that I found *how* I was going to be a big radio personality. And that was to be as honest as possible on the air. (I also credit Howard Stern with being a huge influence and motivation on me in this way. I've never met Howard, only read his books and seen his movie, but I owe a lot to him because he was really the first radio person I had ever known to "put it all out there.")

A given for any radio personality is doing stunts. Stunts are what get people talking about you. The bigger and crazier, the more people will remember it, your show, and the radio station. When I was in Little Rock, someone else had to do the stunts that I devised because I was running the show and couldn't leave the building. Enter my sidekick—Gilligan. That's not his real name. I actually don't remember his real name. If anyone gets a name on the air, I never call them by their real name off the air, so I don't accidentally do it *on* air. Consequently, I have no idea what Gilligan's real first name is. What I do know is that he began his illustrious career in radio as an intern for my show. That's where I plucked him out of obscurity. He had a stoner, surfer voice that made anything he said sound kind of funny. But really the quality that landed him the job of my sidekick was that he would do whatever stupid thing I told him to.

When it comes to stunts, the general rule is the more stupid the better—until you cross that line from stupid into trouble. The problem is, you never really know when you're going to cross it. In Little Rock, there were two Top 40 stations, Alice 107.7 and us. Because it's rare for a town that size to have two stations both playing pop music, the competition was fierce. We went head to head every day. I know; sounds pretty dramatic for two radio stations that both played the Backstreet Boys . . .

One day, though, the other side went too far. I can no longer remember what started the whole series of events that subsequently unfolded, but their night DJ guy had done something that really irritated me. Whatever it was, I know it was stupid—like sticking-an-Alice-107.7-bumper-sticker-on-our-van stupid. But I was a twenty-one-year-old with a chip on my shoulder. Because of my days of being a puny, poor pirate, there is nothing I hate more than being picked on. If I think someone's picking on me then I've got to fight back fifty times worse just to prove to them I'm not weak.

So that's what I did with Alice 107.7. Irritated that they had messed with us, I hatched a diabolical plan to take over their airwaves. It began with Gilligan and me driving across town to Alice as soon as we got off the air. We had exactly one hour to accomplish our mission; I got off the air at 10 P.M., and Alice's nighttime DJ, T. J. Mack, got off the air at 11.

Alice's parent company had recently turned on a brand-new country station in their cluster of radio stations, so the plan was for Gilligan to take one of the cowboy hats lying around in our building (we had our own country station, too) and have him say he worked in their building. Because if you show up wearing a cowboy hat, they're going to let you in, right?

Gilligan—a muscular six-foot-two-inch guy with long hair, gauged ears, and tattoos everywhere—put a cowboy hat on and beat on the door. Watching from my car across the street like some bad private dick, I saw the door open and Gilligan gesture with his hands. Then the person let him in! We were in. *Holy crap.* We were in their radio station!

It was all up to Gilligan now. In preparation for this moment, I had taught him how to use the equipment inside their studio using pictures they had posted to their website. I had scoured the Alice 107.7 website for pictures of their studios, mapped out a diagram, and used them to show Gilligan how to get on the air by explaining what each of the important buttons did and how to locate them. And he was now in their building.

I started driving around Little Rock, waiting to hear from my hidden spy DJ. At around ten forty, Gilligan called me. "I'm in the bathroom," he said. "I'm standing on the toilet so no one sees my feet, so no one knows there's an extra body here."

Gilligan hid in the bathroom and waited. So did I, by the road where people at the station drove out of when they were done. At a little after 11 P.M. I saw T. J. Mack drive right out. Gilligan did what he had been taught to do—he went into the radio station while it was on air, got on the radio station phone, and called my cell phone. Then he took their music three-quarters of the way down (if it goes silent, the engineer gets a call or alarm) and he turned me all the way up on the air. Lastly, he locked the door and left the station.

True to the original plan, I didn't start talking until I was back in front of the station and he had jumped in the car. Then the fun began as we cruised around Little Rock, broadcasting live from my cell phone on our competitor's radio airwaves.

"You don't mess with Bobby Bones at Q100," I said over a Celine Dion song that had been playing. "Everyone listen to Q100! Everyone listen to Q100!"

"Let me talk. Let me talk," Gilligan said, grabbing the phone. "You don't f—"

I tried to pull the phone back in time before he could say what he wanted to, which was, "You don't f— with the Bobby Bones show on Q100." But I didn't get it back before he dropped the F-bomb on a Top 40 station.

Finally someone working in the building got a key and back into the radio station, but not until after we had broadcast for a while. "For a while" felt like three hours while we were driving around. It was probably only a few minutes until they turned the music back up, and Celine Dion drowned us out. Three hours, three minutes. It mattered little. Victory was ours!

Until the next day. I was called into the program director's office at Q100 first thing in the morning. I was told I should be fired and that if I ever did anything like that again, I would never be able to work anywhere in this industry. I didn't get fired, but I got in a whole lot of trouble—trouble that took me beyond my little dreams of living in Little Rock and to a bigger job than I could have ever imagined.

5

STUPID PANTY HOSE TRICKS

Six months after arriving in Little Rock, I was moving again. This time, though, I was moving out of Arkansas for the first time in my life.

Hijacking our competitor's radio broadcast might have put my job in jeopardy, but it launched my career. It didn't make any waves in the general media, but the trade magazines for the radio industry picked up the story with splashy headlines like RADIO ENGAGES IN GUERRILLA WARFARE. All I did was wait in the car for Gilligan, but the articles made me into the Che Guevara of radio.

There was one man, it turns out, who read those pieces and decided, "That's exactly the kind of person I'd like to work for me." Jay Shannon, who programmed KISS 96.7 FM in Austin, Texas, called me up a couple of weeks after the now-infamous incident and, without an interview, offered me nights at the station.

That's how I found myself heading to Austin for a new job. I was nervous, because I'd never even been to Austin before I moved there. I hadn't been anywhere. The sum total of my travels were that vacation I took in high school with Evan's family, my summer roofing with Uncle Bub in Kansas City, and a road trip I took in college with a buddy to Chicago to see a baseball game. We were both huge Cubs fans, so we saved up money, drove thirteen hours to watch a game at Wrigley Field, and then turned right around and drove thirteen hours back to school. That was the farthest I'd ever been. I'd never lived outside of the state—in fact, I never lived more than an hour away from Mountain Pine.

When Jay called to offer me the job, he explained that his night guy was leaving and that although I had been in trouble, it was funny trouble. "We can't believe you did that. We want to hire you, Trouble," he said. "Move to Austin."

So I did. As frightening as it was going somewhere that felt so far from home and everyone, I knew it was the right thing to do for my career. Austin dwarfed Little Rock in size. The move to a much bigger market was a huge one for me and I knew it.

Courtney helped me pack up my stuff and move in what was the worst road trip ever. Courtney drove a truck with a trailer that contained all my stuff, and I was following behind in my little white Pontiac Sunfire with 160,000 miles on it, when we hit a massive ice storm. What normally would have been an eight-hour trip took us twenty-seven hours of ice, snow, eighteen-wheelers that had skidded out, and pure misery. All my stuff was ruined in the move. But I was happy to make it in one piece and have as good a friend as Courtney who was willing to go through hell like that with me.

On the drive into my first day of work at KISS FM, I was bowled over by Austin. Heading north up Congress Avenue, the state capitol looming in front of me, flanked by the tallest towers of glass and steel I had ever seen, I thought, Holy cow! Now *this* is a big city. Little Rock felt very far away. And now, very small.

As soon I walked into the radio station I was greeted by Jay, a friendly man who was not quite old enough to be a father figure but too old to be a big brother. Either way, he took a big chance on me and wound up being one of the most instrumental forces in my career.

From the start of my job, I felt comfortable enough that I talked to Jay almost every day after the show to discuss how it had gone. He never asked me to do this; I always wanted to. He made the radio station an environment I felt comfortable in and wanted to be a part of, which was no easy feat. Jay—who never air-checked me, meaning that he never made me listen to a tape of myself as part of a critique, an excruciating process for a DJ— never made me feel criticized, not one time.

Because of that, I craved his feedback, which was wide-ranging and mostly always right. Even when he knew I was doing wrong, he let me learn from my mistakes. He helped me with the technical aspects of radio, including how to edit down my breaks. Particularly at nights, which is what I started out doing at KISS FM, no one cares about any sort of small talk. Listeners are just waiting for you to get back to the music. "Whatever you think you're going to say, cut it down," he said. "Focus on the point and get to it faster and funnier."

I wanted that kind of advice from him, because I knew he had total confidence in me. The whole management at the station did, it seemed—so much so that only a few months after I had arrived they gave me my own morning show.

This unexpected promotion was precipitated by another job offer, to go to the West Coast. Although I had just started in Austin, I wasn't under contract. And Seattle was an even bigger market than Austin. So I approached the station's general manager, Dusty Black, to explain the situation. "Hey, I think I may go to Seattle," I said. "They're offering me a job, and since I have no contract here, it seems like the right move."

He presided over all six radio stations in our building, heading up everything from programming to sales. Dusty was everybody's boss in Austin. A stout middle-aged guy, he was really pleasant and very Texan, even wearing a cowboy hat at times. Having made a ton of money earlier in radio, he lived in a huge house in the fancy part of town, did his job, but didn't worry about much. I liked Dusty a lot.

"What do you want to stay?" he asked.

Before I moved to Austin, the station had a syndicated morning show that was doing so terrible they cut it. In its place was nothing but music. In that moment, I decided they should put me in that slot.

"I want to do mornings," I said.

"Let me have a couple days to think about it," Dusty said.

Now, I was twenty-two at the time. They should have never given me this job. I was way too young and too dumb. But on Monday, Dusty called me into his office and offered me the morning show for fifty thousand dollars a year.

Not only was I the youngest morning show host of any of the top-fifty rated markets in the country, but I was now rich. Fifty thousand dollars was more money than I had ever imagined I'd be making in my life, and I hadn't even been out of college for three months. With rent worries a thing of the past, I immediately moved out of the apartment I was sharing with a roommate who would leave me little notes like "You owe me seven cents for the slice of bread you took." I'm not kidding. And I would literally find the seven cents that I owed her and put it on the counter. I even referred to her as "the Devil" on the air, which didn't help our living situation much.

In order to put the Devil in context, here is a quick list of the roommates I've had in my life, in descending rank:

Evan: My best friend from high school, with whom I shared
        a college dorm room for about a second. One day I
        came back from work, and he had just moved out. Was
        gone. *WTF?* It was embarrassing to have someone
        just jump ship like that. Looking back, however, I
        was pretty difficult to live with. I had terrible hours in
        college; I woke up early and went to bed really, really
        late. And I didn't party. There was *no* partying in the
        room. When I was there, I needed rest. Still, it was
        pretty crappy to have my best friend bail like that.
Josh: I lived with Josh twice. Once after Evan moved
        out when he was assigned to me. And then in Little
        Rock with his wife. Good dude. Quiet. Quirky. I
        remember when he moved into my dorm room. I wasn't
        there, but all of his stuff was, so I went through his
        closet. It was all slacks and T-shirts. I thought, This guy
        might just be nerdier than I am. And luckily, he was!
        We were perfect roomies.

Matt: Another Henderson State undergrad, he was trying to do radio just like me. After I got him a job at KLAZ, he went by the name Scott Shady. I think he thought he was Eminem's little half cousin. He was my sidekick for a few years, and we would drive back from work every night and prank-call *The John and Jeff Show,* based out of L.A. We also played a lot of Ken Griffey Jr. baseball on my PlayStation.

Courtney: My best friend. TV sharing. Nap sharing. Life sharing. Brother and soul mate. But I was always really jealous of the number of girls he could get. He was as charming as he was good looking. So it seemed like a revolving door of "girls Bobby could never get." That's the only reason he isn't number one.

Jennifer: One of the best humans I have ever met. She was clean and paid rent on time, and her mom knew we were both broke so she bought us groceries once a month. It was the greatest living arrangement ever. When I was sick, she took care of me. When I was hungry, her mom fed me. When the house smelled like a dude, she made sure it didn't. Shout-out to female roommates everywhere. And because of Jennifer, to this day, I still use a loofah.

Oh yeah, back to the start of my radio career . . .

Less than a year after I graduated from college, *The Bobby Bones Show* was born. For a while it was four hours of music, punctuated by a few announcements from me. It was basically the night show, only I had to wake up earlier. The reason I wanted a morning show, however, was because I wanted to talk more. As

I grew more confident I tried to alter the ratio to less music and more talk, but I got pushback from Dusty and Jay. "Music gets ratings; you don't," they said. "Music's proven; you're not."

They were right. But I continued to push for more time making jokes, taking calls, and discussing current events, and slowly the ratings got a little better and a little better. Although Jay, Dusty, and I struggled over this issue for years, I was able to build, and slowly outpace, the station's ratings historically during the morning. And when you start outpacing the ratings, your argument becomes a whole lot stronger.

I'd like to claim total responsibility for the improving ratings, but a lot of the credit had to go to my new sidekick, Lunchbox.

Ah, Lunchbox. Where do I begin? I guess with how we met. We were—naturally—at a bar. (Lunchbox is a party animal. In our little group, he's the wild one. If there's alcohol around he's going to drink it. And he's going to have a great time.) I was doing a station event that he showed up to because his sister knew my morning show. Lunchbox, who wasn't yet Lunchbox but Dan Chappell.

An Austin native, he was working as a delivery driver for Jason's Deli when I met him. He was really loud and obnoxious, and funny—more loud and obnoxious than funny, if I'm honest, but that somehow made him funnier. At the time, *The Bobby Bones Show* was just an intern named Jill and me. Looking to add people to the mix, I had a feeling about this guy and approached Lunchbox: "Hey, man, would you want to come and arm-wrestle female rugby players tomorrow?"

"Sure," he said.

Lunchbox showed up the next morning along with the rugby players, who had arrived to promote a local event. I thought

Lunchbox would probably get dominated and that'd be funny enough. But Lunchbox dialed it up. Although he lost to all the team members, he still talked trash to each and every one of them.

"You all got lucky!"

"If we wrestled again, I'd crush you."

"Were you wearing some kind of cream? I couldn't get a grip."

"CHEATERS!"

And he kept on and on.

I thought it was the funniest thing that after getting killed by all these women, this guy still had no problem running his mouth. He had all the makings of a great sidekick: funny, game, and totally shameless. So I asked him to come back, again and again, until I was able to hire him part-time. Because I couldn't afford to hire him full-time, he worked a second job at Sam's Club.

That the man who was on the radio with me every day was also a stock boy at Sam's Club pretty much sums up the ethos of those early days of *The Bobby Bones Show*. It was then Lunchbox; my intern, Jill; and me—and we were all kids. At twenty-three, I was the elder statesman. Lunchbox was twenty-two, and Jill, twenty-one, was still in college! She would leave the studio at eight o'clock to make it to school in time for class. It was nuts they let us have a show. The one thing we had going for us: we were cheap.

We worked on a bare-bones budget. Lunchbox didn't even have a microphone in the studio. So we sent him to the streets and he did all the bits on his cell phone. He was and is a total team player, willing to do anything at any point. We did all kinds of stuff to him. Once we wrapped him in bubble wrap and threw him out of a moving car. Another time we had him climb a huge water tower. There was something we called Pain Day, where we would do all these painful things to Lunchbox like putting electric shock probes on him, giving him a body wax, or having him walk across hot coals. We challenged him to see how much butter he could eat in an hour, staged a naked run in the city, and had a competition to see who could put the most clothespins on their face. He even married a listener (who was paid a hundred dollars for the honor), though the marriage was annulled the next day.

If I had needed someone to dress up in a clown outfit and run down Sixth Street with two sheep and a casket, he would have said, "Okay! When?" I mean, for Pete's sake, he robbed a store for me. Well, he didn't *really* rob it. Actually he didn't rob it at all. Here's what happened.

In July 2004, after about a year of the morning show, I was watching some old show on PBS late at night where a guy wearing panty hose on his head goes up to people on the street and starts talking to them like his face isn't smushed down by a woman's stocking. I thought it was hilarious and immediately my mind went to, What if we put panty hose on Lunchbox? Instead of talking to people on the street, I imagined Lunchbox walking into a convenience store with panty hose on his head, like how robbers do when they are going to hold it up. Except Lunchbox obviously wasn't going to rob the store. He'd just walk in and buy some gum or something. That was the bit.

The next morning around 7 A.M., after Lunchbox, Jill, and I chewed over the events of the day—John Kerry tapping John Edwards as his running mate and Britney Spears getting engaged to K-Fed—Lunchbox drove down South Congress Avenue to a convenience store. Using his cell phone to give listeners the play-by-play of the gag, he put the panty hose over his face, walked into the store, and purchased a pack of gum.

We just wanted to see what kind of reaction he would get. From his reports via cell phone, it wasn't much. The clerk rang up his gum for $1.09 and that was it. We were wrong, though. The reaction, as it turned out, was not pleasant.

While Lunchbox was driving back to the studio, four or five cop cars pulled him over. With their guns pointed at him, the policemen shouted for him to put his hands up. This was no speeding-violation stop. Unbeknownst to any of us, the convenience store clerk had hit the silent alarm under the cash register when he saw a guy with panty hose enter. When the police arrived he described the "getaway" car, and Lunchbox was caught within minutes.

The officers threw Lunchbox in the back of a cop car and drove to the radio station, where they summoned me. When I got outside I saw employees from the station trying to enter the parking lot to park their cars for work, except they couldn't because cop cars with flashing lights were blocking it. I ran up to the cops, who said they were going to arrest me, and that's when I saw Lunchbox handcuffed in the back of a cop car. *Holy crap.*

In the end I was not arrested because there was nothing to charge me with. I went back inside to finish the show, or as much as I could before I got pulled off the air. Meanwhile Lunchbox called me from jail. His voice is so deep, and he has such a thick accent, that people who only know him from the radio are always surprised that he's just some skinny white guy. He sounds so big, but he's not. Just a skinny dude—and now he was in jail, charged with making a terrorist threat, a Class A misdemeanor punishable by up to a year in jail and up to a four-thousand-dollar fine.

I had to call his parents. It was an awesome conversation. "Sir, so we did this segment where your son put panty hose on his head . . ."

Before I left work that day, I was suspended indefinitely. And Dusty, my general manager, had to cut his vacation short and fly back to town because of this. I felt awful, but Jay reassured me (even though he had moved to San Antonio to work for a different station by this point). "As long as this doesn't blow up into too much of a story, you'll be fine," he said. "We'll get through this."

Jay had believed in me enough to let me fail from day one. He understood I was going to learn the most by messing up. Before the panty hose incident, we did a dumb segment on April Fool's Day where I said, "Hey, I'm going to get on the air and act like we're doing casting for a Justin Timberlake video. Let's see who shows up. And whoever does, we'll put their pictures on our website." Then I waited about half an hour and actually made the fake announcement about casting for a JT video. Girls dropped whatever they were doing and showed up at the station for a chance to be in the "music video," and just as I promised, we put their pictures up on the website under a banner that read, APRIL FOOL'S: WE GOT YOU.

One of those ladies wound up suing us. Now, usually if a program director hears the word "lawsuit," they go ballistic. But, you know, Jay never got too upset about it. He just kind of handled it. Giving me room to make my own mistakes was the biggest vote of confidence I could imagine receiving.

I was grateful to Jay for it, and clearly took full advantage in terms of messing up. "As long as it doesn't blow up too big," he had said after Lunchbox was arrested. Well, when I say that the panty hose incident "blew up," I mean it *blew up*. That night every local newscast flashed Lunchbox's mug shot and the *Bobby Bones Show* logo. When the radio station's attorneys went down to the police station to bail Lunchbox out, they had to take him out the back so he wouldn't be overrun by the throng of TV reporters and cameramen waiting outside the jail.

It didn't stop there. The next morning, it was on the front page of the *Austin Statesman*. "We are taking this very seriously," police spokesman Kevin Buchman told the *Statesman*. "People at convenience stores, banks and other places of business are on heightened alert, and some business owners have been known to carry weapons. Trying to pull off a prank endangered the life of not only himself but anybody else who might have been in the store."

It must have been the slowest news day in the history of news, because the Associated Press picked it up. And anytime the AP picks up a story, it goes to everyone who subscribes to the newswire service all over the world. Dusty had to release a written statement: "KISS FM does not endorse behavior that may endanger the public or our employees, and we take these matters very seriously."

The story continued to grow as it hit CNN, Yahoo's news site, and every outlet imaginable. While watching a late-night talk show, I saw a segment on stupid news—and there we were.

It wasn't just late-night audiences who were laughing at us. Every other radio show in Austin and beyond mocked us and spun the story out until it turned into Lunchbox robbing a convenience store while wearing a ski mask, and the both of us getting fired. Lunchbox hadn't robbed anyone or worn a ski mask—and we weren't fired. Not yet, at least.

We were, however, suspended without pay until further

notice. KISS FM's management was furious with me. As one week of suspension turned into two weeks, I had no clue what was going to happen. There were court dates, attorney meetings, and backroom dealings with radio executives while I was left to spend all day sitting on my couch, growing what I could of a beard and contemplating what a moron I had been.

It was a terrible idea. A terrible idea. Not because I was probably going to get fired, but because Lunchbox could have died. The convenience store clerk could have pulled a gun out and shot him. How had I not thought that through before? Had I been so concerned about stunts and ratings that I was willing to put another person's life in jeopardy? What a selfish jerk.

The truth is that most of the kinds of stunts done on the radio have an element of danger to them. Like I said, what makes something go from being a funny bit to a bad idea is if something bad happens. That's it. Years after this, some radio DJs I know at the local station in Sacramento held a contest in which selected listeners competed to see how much water they could drink without peeing. Now, this is a bit that a thousand radio stations have done. But in this case, the twenty-eight-year-old mother of three children who won the contest was found dead of water intoxication a few hours later. Her husband was eventually awarded $16.5 million in a wrongful death lawsuit he brought against the radio station.

It's never anyone's intention for someone to get hurt in these gags. I knew it wasn't mine. But even if Lunchbox didn't get hurt, I'd probably ruined our careers. During our suspension, we knew it was bad while playing golf. (Now that I was making a smooth 50K a year, I felt like I needed to learn golf. You know, like the other millionaires.) While Lunchbox and I were playing, we overheard one of the men teeing up before us say to the other, "Did you hear about those radio DJs that robbed the store?"

Lunchbox and I looked at each other in disbelief.

"You've got to be kidding me," I said. "Even old people know about this?"

My mistake spanned all audiences and all platforms.

In that time, I went to a really negative place. It was awful. I slept on the couch when I slept at all. In one stupid move, I had gone from a celebrated young radio personality on the rise to a typical twenty-three-year-old doing the kind of dumb thing twenty-three-year-olds do. I was convinced I was going to be fired and truly believed I would never get a job in radio again.

I was so depressed that for the first time since my grandma passed away during my junior year of college, I finally mourned her. I didn't have any family members I could talk to about what was going on. My sister and I had fallen out of touch. She had her own personal drama happening as well as a baby, so we weren't close at the time. And my mom continued to struggle with her addictions. If I ever did speak to her on the phone it was because she needed something from me. Plus, my grandmother and I had been closer than my mom and I ever were.

That's why when I was a little kid I was always terrified she was going to die. She wasn't sick or even that old, but I was scared of losing her. Preoccupied with this thought, one day I asked my grandma what happens after you die. A very religious woman, she believed that if you were good you went to heaven; if you were bad you went to hell. She also said that the dead can reappear on earth as angels to protect the living. Now, it was hard for me to believe in angels running around, since I was the kind of kid who was told at five that Santa Claus was a fake just so I understood why there weren't presents. But I would have believed in Santa Claus, the Easter Bunny, and anything else if it ensured I'd never lose my grandma. So I asked her, when she was dying, if there really was some sort of system for reaching back to the living, could she please give me a sign. "You will know," she said.

There was a moment during my suspension in Austin when I didn't think I could get any lower. I was in turmoil. Trying to figure out what I was supposed to do as a human being on this planet, I had never felt more alone. My entire identity was (and still is, for the most part) my job. And this is coming from a person who had spent most of his life alone.

"Okay, Grandma," I said out loud inside my empty apartment. "We had this deal that if you were out there, you would reach out to me in some way. And you haven't."

All of a sudden (meaning anywhere from five to forty-five seconds later; I didn't time it), my guitar, which had belonged to my grandmother and had been leaning against the wall, came crashing to the ground. It was an old cheap instrument that has since fallen apart, but I had inherited it as a keepsake from my grandma after she died. I'm a bad guitar player, but when I played on her guitar I was reminded of how she taught herself well enough to play in church. She wasn't a musician but got to the point where everyone knew her as one. So if there was going to be one object that embodied my grandma, it would have been that guitar—and the damn thing fell over!

The logical part of me doesn't believe the ghost of my grandmother pushed that guitar over to send me a sign. (I have a weird thing about ghosts—whether it's my grandmother or anyone else I have known who died, I don't want them watching over me, because that means they're seeing when I go to the bathroom, pick my nose, hook up with a girl—or, mostly, hook up with myself. If they see all that, I'd prefer they didn't exist!) But wasn't it really strange that her guitar fell over right after I called to her? The idea freaked me out so much that I inspected the apartment to see if there was something that could have tipped the guitar over—the air conditioner turning on or a gust of wind through an open window. But there was nothing.

I completely don't "believe" that it was her, but there's a part of me that can't write it off completely. There's nothing to convince me either way, so I have to make peace with it. What I believe is that I'm going to do as much good for others as I can, and then we'll just see what happens.

A brief time after the panty hose incident, all the charges against Lunchbox were dropped. In the end, we were stupid but we didn't break the law in any way. Shortly after the legal resolution, I got the call to come into the office to meet with Dusty, with no hint as to what kind of conversation was going to take place. The Imperial March music from *Star Wars* played in my head.

"Issue an apology," he said. "You're not fired. You'll start back on Monday."

We were back on the air.

I was relieved, grateful, and deeply humbled. All of that took the show to a new level. I was a better person because of the huge lesson I had learned, and that made the show better.

While we had been off the air, our getting fired was a news story. When it was announced we were coming back, the news story was we were *not* getting fired. Our show before the panty hose stunt had been only moderately successful—probably ranked ninth or tenth in Austin—but it was not anywhere near the top. On the day I came back on air, we had more listeners than ever before tuning in to hear me make an apology. People love apologies.

They are crazy for them. It doesn't matter what you are apologizing for—or if they know what you're apologizing for. Much later, when I was already working in Nashville, I did a whole social media campaign of me apologizing. For what? Who knew. I told the people on my show, "Let's do this bit. It'll blow up." I shot a video of me saying, "I just want to come on and say I'm really sorry for what happened. I should have never done that. I just hope you guys can forgive me . . ."

This amorphous apology garnered thousands of comments. Thousands. Some people wanted to know, "What did he do?" "What happened?" But soon people were assigning great meaning to it. "That's really great of you." "It is much appreciated." Taking responsibility for the bad things you've done by admitting you're at fault is seen as a virtue, even if no one has a clue what you're talking about.

So lots of curious new listeners tuned in to *The Bobby Bones Show* and heard me say I was really sorry for the panty hose stunt, how it was very stupid of me, and that I'd never do anything like it again—and they wound up hanging around. In the next three months our show climbed to number one, where it pretty much remained for the next decade.

It was amazing to think how close I had come to ruining my life at twenty-three years old. We had actually considered sending Lunchbox to make a deposit into the bank with panty hose over his head. To this day it makes me sick just thinking about that. Okay, truth time: Lunchbox was on his way to a bank, where he also planned to wear the panty hose, when he was arrested at the gas station! Thankfully, I had a great guy for a general manager. He didn't take a reactionary stance and call for my head but instead gave me a second chance. For that I am forever grateful, which I showed by naming my dog after him.

Now, anyone who has listened to my show for a minute knows my dog is the great love of my life. I love animals and wanted a dog, but it had to be small because I lived in a tiny apartment and had no money. The Staffordshire bull terrier breed was perfect because they are small, but unlike with a Pomeranian or Chihuahua I could still be a self-respecting man (at least in my mind) walking one. The dog I adopted was the runt of a litter of Staffordshire bull terriers from a puppy mill. He was really too small to take away from his mother, but because the breeders had been busted, all the dogs were separated. When I got him, he was so small he could fit in my hand. There was no doubt what his name had to be. "I named my firstborn after you," I told Dusty. "He just happens to be a dog."

6

BONES BARED

"Hey, are you the guy from the radio?" a pretty girl with a big smile said.

It was a regular old Saturday in 2005 and I was in Culver's, a burger and custard chain, eating dinner solo while I waited to have my tires replaced at the shop right up the street. To be fair, new tires or not, I'd have probably been eating alone anyway. I do most things alone. Eat. Go to the movies. Make love. You know, all the stuff you wish someone else was participating in.

Anyway, the woman standing in front of my table said my name, startling me midbite, since—it might shock some of you to learn—I'm not used to pretty girls coming up to me.

"Yeah," I said in a reply that was typical of my eloquence.

She then offered me some coupons for free ice cream, which at first I thought were something she wanted me to purchase.

And I probably would have, if it included some of her company for the next few minutes, because even though I do everything alone, that doesn't mean I want to. But no, she was offering them to me for free. And that was it. We exchanged nice-to-meet-yous, and I had some small pieces of paper that each promised me one free ice cream cone.

That was Amy, now my radio cohost and one of my best friends. She is the person who, at this point in my life, probably knows more about me than anyone else in the world. She is quite possibly the friendliest person I've ever met. But to be fair, she did get those ice cream coupons for free, because her friend's family owned the store.

The next time I saw Amy, who I still didn't know as Amy, was not long after at the Barton Creek Mall, where we were holding an event for listeners. The purpose of our being there was to see if we could find someone to add to the show's mix. We weren't really looking for a new cohost. It was more of a let's-see-if-there's-anyone-interesting-out-there kind of thing where tons of people usually showed up. As the night went on, we met a lot of cool folks, but none who really stood out. We were about to wrap it up when Amy, the same girl from Culver's, appeared. She hadn't been standing in line for hours and didn't have some kind of bit planned. In fact, as I learned later from her friends, she had to be convinced to show up at the mall after her job was over that day. But she said hi again, and we talked for a little while. And then we went our separate ways.

I didn't offer her a trial on the show, but there was something warm and appealing about Amy that stood out from the crowd. The truth is, the event was sort of bogus, since I only ever hire my friends. If I'm going to spend as much time with other people in such a tiny space as you have to in order to do a radio show, I need to know them, like them, and trust them. Amy wasn't my friend, but I wanted her to be. So I set out to see if we could become friends. Over the next five months or so, I friend-auditioned her. We went to dinner occasionally or caught a movie, including the latest Pixar release, *Cars*. Our outings were always something silly like that, so they wouldn't be misconstrued in any way as a date. We were both single, but I was only in it for friendship business. Is that a term? Not sure, but Amy sure succeeded in it.

Months later I invited Amy to sit in on the show. This time, though, I was inviting my friend, a Texas A&M alum and granite salesperson whom I met after she offered me coupons for free ice cream at Culver's. She nailed it and I offered her a job.

I wasn't wrong about my instinct: listeners took to her instantly, and our rapport was so good, many began to speculate that we were in love with each other. Okay, here would be a good place to clear up any misconceptions. THERE HAS NEVER BEEN ANYTHING ROMANTIC WITH US, EVER. NOT ONCE. After Amy started on the show, she got married to the dude she was actually in love with—a pilot who served twelve years in the air force. (So yeah, even if I did like her like that, I wouldn't have had a chance anyway.)

Amy and I are just good friends. That's really it. I wouldn't believe it myself if I didn't know it was true, because she and I are the exception to the rule about male-female relationships. See, a girl can be a friend to a guy. No problem. She can have an absolutely platonic friendship with a guy who is good looking, bad looking, funny, nerdy, foreign, blond. Doesn't matter. Women have the awesome ability to just be awesome. And friendly. They can be your friend.

This is not the case for guys. Guys *cannot* be legitimate friends with a female who is attractive to them. Now, guys, you may be reading this saying, "This is such crap, I have a female friend." Before I continue writing, let me remind you that I have a penis. Not anything to brag about, but I am a dude. So I know how we work, how we think, how we're wired. At least I know how I think and how all my friends think. The evidence for my next proclamation is rather substantial—and it's not pleasant, but here it is. If a guy *isn't* attracted to a girl, he can be her friend. If a guy *is* attracted to a girl, he is just waiting for her to have sex with him. There *can* be friendship inside of that. It's not *just* about sex. But every dude with a female friend who is hot is just waiting . . . and don't buy it if he refuses to admit it. If you're married, it's all good. He'll wait. If he's married, cool, he'll still wait (or he won't). If you're both in a relationship, the time just isn't right yet. Or it may never be. But eventually, just maybe, it will be.

As soon as Amy joined the show, everyone loved her. I mean EVERYONE LOVED (LOVES) AMY. It's annoying sometimes. She really is that great. Asdlkfhal;sfjdslf;ja. That shows you how annoyed I am.

The only person who did *not* take to Amy was Lunchbox. He really didn't like her. And she really didn't like him, either. Just as he's an incredibly loyal guy, Lunchbox is equally territorial. He couldn't stand someone new—particularly a girl—homing in on his turf. It quickly seemed like his new job description was to be mean to Amy. If he wasn't making misogynist jokes, then he was trying to block her out of segments on the show. Literally, not letting her talk. If Amy got anywhere near one of his beloved subjects—like sports—he verbally trampled her. He didn't want someone barging in on his turf, which I understand because I'm pretty touchy myself about that kind of thing. But Lunchbox took it to such an extreme that Amy was miserable. In the early period of her joining the show, she cried a lot and almost quit a few times—including right after the now-infamous candy incident.

It was Valentine's Day 2008 when someone sent a tube filled with chocolates to the office. We started chatting about who the box was addressed to, with Amy saying it was for all of us and me arguing that it had my name on it. But what started off as friendly banter about a harmless subject quickly morphed into us ganging up on Amy. Then Lunchbox went into an area of particular vulnerability for her: food. A number of times on air, Amy had openly discussed her history with bulimia earlier in her life.

"Do you see how angry Amy gets when you take food away from her?" Lunchbox said, taking the conversation into hostile territory.

It was one step too far. And we go too far sometimes on the show; we are normal humans. Sometimes things get out of hand. But this was just really mean.

"Eat the stamp," Lunchbox said to Amy. "Eat that address label so you know who it was really sent to."

"I hope whoever takes over my job is prepared," Amy said.

It was getting ugly fast, and there was no dialing it back now. Microphones up. Keep it real, right?

But her self-defense only egged on Lunchbox, who continued to mock her, now not only for her food issues but also for her complaining about her job. As his tone grew louder and more aggressive, Amy became quieter, her eyes welling up with tears.

Most human beings would give it a rest at that point, but not Lunchbox; he dumped the candy that had been in the tube all over her head.

"Here is a sucker so you can suck on it while you cry," he said.

Refusing to acknowledge Lunchbox directly, which was her best weapon against him, she said to me, "He is such a jerk."

On air, she held it together, claiming she was letting the whole thing roll off her back and that she wasn't going to cry. But as soon as the show was done, she walked out of the studio and quit. She was done. At least for the next hour or so. Then she calmed down. That day was such a mess, I had to ask Amy if I had all the details down when I was writing this chapter. And it all started with something so stupid and small.

The bad blood between these two had gone far enough. I had to mediate and make them at least relax around each other. Peace didn't come immediately (or even close to immediately; I think it actually took a couple of years). But finally they worked it out, because they're both good people. Though obnoxious and loud, fundamentally Lunchbox is a really good guy. We've been together longer than anyone else on that show—and remember, he went to jail for me.

Amy's just a good person—no caveats. In all ways, from her faith to the connections she makes with others, Amy is really one of the best people I've ever met. She is definitely the most devout person I know. But she doesn't preach and is never in your face about anything. She leads by example.

There are only about four or five people who I can honestly say have really motivated me to be a better person—and Amy is one of them. Just like hanging around great musicians makes you want to play better, or being around funny people makes you want to be funnier, being around good people makes you want to be a better person.

After Amy traveled to Haiti on a mission there, she became very involved with the country and eventually created her own nonprofit called TEEMHaiti, which works to improve the lives of a wide variety of Haitians—including providing hunger relief. Listening to her talk about the struggles people were going through down there, you couldn't help be moved to do something. There are a lot of people here in the U.S. struggling, too, but when your friend finds a passion, it also becomes important to you. In that same way, many of my projects have become important to her. Later on, when we moved to Nashville, I helped Amy with an event where volunteers came out to pack up meals for the orphanage in Port-au-Prince that Amy supports. We wanted to see if we could break the Guinness World Record for most hunger relief meals packaged in one hour by a team (just because we were doing something good doesn't mean we couldn't turn it into a stunt), and we did, with 530,064 meals packed in forty-five minutes.

That's just one example of so many ways Amy brings positivity into life, even during its darkest moments, like when her mom, Judy, was diagnosed with cancer in 2012. Amy and her sister, Cristi, are both really close to their mom and to each other. They were devastated when they learned of their mom's illness. But Amy heeded her mom's message to "choose joy," so much so that she had JOY tattooed on her wrist in her mother's handwriting. Before Judy passed away in 2014, we decided to do something called "Pimpin' Joy Week" on *The Bobby Bones Show*, where we were looking not for donations or money but for stories that "inspire, influence, and encourage people to Choose Joy."

People still call in to the show almost every day to tell us how they are "pimpin' joy." As I write this, I just had dinner, and my meal was paid for by two listeners from Houston who didn't hang around for a thank-you but just wrote "pimpinjoy" on my receipt, which was just awesome. However, they paid for it before I ordered pie. So I still paid for the pie. Just a few more minutes and I'd have gotten some pie pimpinjoyed, too!

Amy doesn't just make me a better person; she also makes me a better radio personality. She's so real that she challenges me to stay real. As our radio show continued to grow in popularity, it would have been natural for me to slip into a fake image of who I thought I needed to be, which ultimately would have become stale to listeners. Sitting every morning next to someone who wears her heart on her sleeve, I couldn't live with myself if I didn't maintain the same level of honesty.

Honesty is kind of the through line for everyone who wound up joining *The Bobby Bones Show*. Oh, and also that Lunchbox hated everybody when they first joined the gang. He hated Amy. He hated Ray. He hated Eddie. It's happened every single time, with every single person that comes in. But as with any family, I always say, "No one's going anywhere. You're just all going to have to sort it out."

A family is what *The Bobby Bones Show* is—an insular family, because I hardly ever bring in new people. And the new people I do bring in aren't strangers, because they're either friends of mine or people who started as interns who spent a year or two working with us for free before joining for good.

Part of the reason my standards were so high for new people was that I would have felt like I had let the team down if I'd brought in someone who wasn't strong. Ray—a producer who cuts all the audio for the broadcast from a glassed-in room where I can see him while I'm doing the show—was a bulldog of a worker as soon as he arrived. He was an intern, but an older one. Already out of college and working, he just decided one day that he wanted to get into radio. He wasn't even officially an intern, to be honest; he just showed up. And showed up. And showed up. There were other producers who he was outworking like crazy, and he wasn't getting paid. And I'm loyal to my people as long as they're strong and keep the team going—and Ray was very strong.

Eddie, a family man with a wife and two children, was my old television producer and has been a fast friend for over ten years now. He's half of my comedy/music band, the Raging Idiots, and we spend pretty much seven days a week together—five in the studio doing radio and two on the road doing concerts on the weekends.

I should probably give a brief history of the Raging Idiots, which was first the name of my high school band. Well, actually, not the original name. We started out as the Concubine Kings. But after realizing we couldn't play church events with that name, I changed it to the Raging Idiots. What? I was sixteen years old. We probably played six gigs, pulling in about twenty dollars total, before giving up. That wasn't a bad run, considering I was the lead singer—and I couldn't sing.

Later when I was on the radio, I started playing little songs on my guitar that I made up, à la Adam Sandler. They were funny little segments. At least I thought they were funny. For these segments, I resurrected the Raging Idiots. I became Bobby Bones and the Raging Idiots, even though I was the only one playing. There were no other members. I just turned into a band when I picked up my guitar. My "band" got its first real gig when I opened up for Toya (look her up), who put out her debut single "I Do!!" in 2001. They needed someone to kill twenty minutes before she went on, so I went onstage in Little Rock and played a song I wrote called "Dream Girl."

> *I have a dream girl on my mind.*
> *She is so perfect she is so fine.*

Yes, the song was really that dumb (my songs still are). But a girl actually came up to me after the show to say she liked my song, and we made out. That was my entrance to music, and I was hooked. But that was pretty much it for my career as a musician—other than a brief moment in 2005 when I recorded a song with Olympic gymnast (and aspiring pop singer) Carly Patterson. For the remix of the song called "Temporary Life," I was billed under the rap name Captain Caucasian. Oddly enough, the song got some radio play, so I did a few shows as Captain Caucasian and the Raging Idiots.

But the *real* Raging Idiots didn't get going until Eddie joined *The Bobby Bones Show* and we began doing parodies of current hit songs on the radio (he on guitar and me "singing"). The Raging Idiots were good for ratings, and it was fun to write and play again. We really had no aspirations of doing anything other than sitting in the studio and making fun of songs until Amy had a charity event and needed a "band" to play. After that, we started playing shows. But not for money, though, since we donated all the proceeds to charity. Driving hundreds of miles every weekend, we went everywhere from California to North Carolina to D.C. to Wisconsin to Texas, only to be back on the air Monday. Before we knew it, we had raised $30,000 for various charities, then \$300,000, then \$750,000, until we eventually hit \$1 million! It was fun and meaningful but also exhausting being on the road that much. But I have nothing on Eddie, who does it with a wife and two kids. So although he's perpetually late (on tour and on the show), I get past it because I know he's a stand-up dude.

Sometimes I think the best thing about my show is that I get to work with friends, people who I hired because they are trustworthy, interesting, and enjoyable to be around. But none of them were radio guys. We were the top-rated morning show in Austin and syndicated in five other cities—and no one other than me had any experience or background in radio. Like I mentioned, Amy sold granite. Lunchbox was delivering for Jason's Deli. Eddie was a TV producer. Ray was a . . . well, I'm not sure what Ray was. He did some telemarketing. . . . I love the fact that everyone on *The Bobby Bones Show* was a real person, but it means that I have to work behind the scenes, too, in order to preserve that authenticity.

I put four or five hours of preparation into a four- or five-hour show that to listeners sounds (hopefully) like we're just talking about whatever we want, whenever we want. So the whole radio show is planned out, minute to minute, but if it ever sounds like that, then it means I've done something wrong.

My trick to making our conversations sound spontaneous and not scripted is simple: I'm the only one on the show who knows what topics are on the table for the day. Amy, Lunchbox, and Eddie have no idea what subjects I'm going to talk about or when I might bring up something they've said. Keeping them in the dark keeps them normal people, talking like normal people do.

I always keep a running list of discussion topics that I gather from all over the place. It could be a heartwarming story I read on the Associated Press about a blind couple that got married after their guide dogs brought them together, or something I overheard at a party (just kidding, I don't go to parties—it was on the Internet) about how the nutrition bars Amy always eats aren't actually healthy. Waking up with a pimple after breaking my diet, I put the question of whether sugar causes pimples up for debate. The status of my dating life is an evergreen topic.

Everyone on the show knows if they send me something, beware, because I can use it on the show at any time. I may use it next week, I may use it today, or I may use it never. I plan every second of the show (although it never goes 100 percent exactly as planned). I know what we're going to hit and when we're going to hit it, and the crew all follow my lead. If I need forty-five seconds to read something quietly, they sit quietly and let me refocus on what we're about to do. Then Ray walks in and hands me a sheet to start reading—read, read, read, read—and in ten seconds we're back on live and the whole gang is animated again.

It's not an act. None of them could act to save their lives. My bringing stuff up at random is how we keep it loose and sounding like the big group of friends we are. The realness isn't always laughs; it has been known to veer into on-air crying and screaming matches (usually involving Lunchbox). But it's like a marriage—not that I really know, since I've never even been close to married—in that we're together so much that we're bound to get on each other's nerves. I mean, when you spend at minimum five hours a day at arm's length to another person, talking about everything under the sun, there are going to be times you can't stand each other.

For the most part, though, we care for each other. The rawness of real emotion—either good or bad—has always been the main draw of the show. That's part of the reason why after one of the worst moments in my life, when I really thought I was going to be killed, my immediate instinct was to do a show. The early morning of September 29, 2009, started out like every other morning for the past five years since I had begun broadcasting from Austin. After waking up at 3 A.M. (yup, that's what I mean by early morning), I would hop out of bed and practically right into the car to arrive at work no later than 4 A.M. I always parked at the bottom of a big hill, atop which was the radio station. There was never anyone in the parking lot, on my walk up the hill, or in the building where I spent the next hour or two before we went on air reading up on the news and plotting out the show.

On this morning, after walking the hill like always, I got close to the building's front door, which you have to put a code into and then pull open after the beep, a process that takes a second.

That's when I heard someone say, "Hey, Bones."

I turned around and there was a man in a ski mask, who started running toward me.

I don't know how I didn't hear him or see him, but all of a sudden he was charging at me with something in his hand that I couldn't quite identify. I didn't have a long time to look, anyhow, because there was a man with a mask chasing me.

I kicked off the flip-flops I was wearing and ran as fast as I could. I never considered fighting him. I tore down an outdoor alley that was about sixty yards long. I can still run pretty fast. I'm still in decent shape even though I sit in a studio most of the time. I was running as fast as I could, but he was on my heels. I still had my backpack on with a computer inside—the same backpack I still carry today. "Well, this is holding me down," I thought to myself as I threw it off my back, hoping he just wanted to rob me and would stop for the bag.

Nope.

The guy in the ski mask passed the backpack and continued to chase me. I ran until I hit a concrete barrier. Fueled by adrenaline and the desire not to die, I jumped over the barrier. But the ground on the other side was much farther down than on the side I had come from, so I wiped out when I jumped and smacked my knee and shoulder. I was in pain.

Luckily, a car pulled up right at that moment, otherwise the guy definitely would have gotten to me. When he saw the lights of the car, the man in the ski mask stopped, turned around, and ran away.

The man in the car, Matt, an engineer and producer who worked at another station in the building, gave me a look like *WTF just happened to you?*

I went into the building, got some ice for my knee, and called 911. The cops showed up and started to ask me questions for the report about what happened, but at four thirty in the morning I looked at the officers and told them we had to stop the interview. "Guys, I have to go on the air at five o'clock," I said.

So I hopped on the air and opened up the microphone.

"Hey, everybody. Good morning," I said. "Welcome to the show. You guys are not going to believe what just happened to me. I just got jumped."

About forty-five seconds into the story, I started crying on the air. I wasn't sad, but I couldn't control my reactions. Whatever had just happened had built up such a mass of anxiety and feeling that everything came pouring out when I began talking about it.

It was a similar reaction to how I responded after I competed in a few triathlons. Each time I finished one of those, I experienced a release that wasn't about happiness or sadness, just raw emotion. This crying was physical, a real breaking down. And the listeners heard each sob.

I eventually settled myself down, finished telling the story, and then finished the show. When I was done, the cops continued their questioning of me. Except now they started to act as if the whole thing was a prank. "Are you sure it wasn't one of your buddies?" one asked. "You set this up?"

I'd never been so pissed off in my life. I almost died and the members of the Austin PD were treating me like I was making it up? (Later, a rival radio station accused me of the same thing.) But they didn't have to take my word for it; there was surveillance footage of the incident that we watched together later. Watching that video footage was almost scarier than the real thing. You could see the guy waiting for me, which is why I didn't see him. What he had in his hand turned out to be a knife—and on his belt he had a pair of rubber gloves!

A couple of weeks later, the cops showed up at the radio station and started beating on the window of my studio. "We need you to come outside and identify this guy," one said through the glass.

Since the attack, I had hardly slept. Just like when I had a gun held to my head outside the Electric Cowboy in Little Rock, I had vivid nightmares in which I lived out the terror of the moment right in the confines of my bedroom.

"Not doing it," I said.

I didn't want to leave my studio, because he definitely knew who *I* was. If I identified him, and in the best-case scenario, he went to jail, how long would he serve? A month? Six months? And then, he'd be back out . . .

"We really need you to identify this guy," the officer said. "If you don't, he could do this to someone else."

Oh man, how could I say no to that?

"Fine."

I left the station and got in the back of the cop car. We drove up to another cop car where the police had the suspect handcuffed and standing facing the car. When my window was right beside the man, they shone a light right in his face. I didn't know his face, because he'd had a ski mask on, but I said to the officers that his body type looked exactly like the body type of the guy that chased me. That was the last I ever saw or heard of him.

Even if I had seen the guy's face, I don't know how much help I could have been. The whole incident was such a blur. I couldn't even think straight until after the show that morning. Because of that and the fact that I was so emotional on air, a lot of my friends and the public said I shouldn't have done the show right away. I should have taken the day off, they said. But I think that's always been the appeal of the show—conveying my experiences exactly as they are and without a filter. That realness and rawness is what connects to listeners. The attempted attack was no different. If I had taken the day off, I wouldn't have been able to capture what really happened and put it out there. That, for me, is the best therapy.

My little sister and me. I was probably around twenty-five in this picture. Or five. Probably five, but I could be wrong.

That's a cute kid. And I bet there are a lot of socks in those gifts around me.

Below: I won a poetry contest in fifth grade. The first lines of my poem were "If I had a wish, there would be world peace. I'd stop all the wars, there'd be no more deceased."

I was in ninth grade at this time but still hadn't grown yet. It was football game day, so I had to wear a tie. Also, check out my sweet mullet.

Reflections Winner
1st Place Bobby Estell

I was a five-star wide receiver recruited out of Mountain Pine High School. And by "five-star," I mean, very mediocre.

I had sweet bangs. I also did all the school announcements. But mostly I had sweet bangs.

HOLY CRAP.

I GRADUATED COLLEGE.

THE FIRST PERSON IN MY FAMILY!

A Polaroid of my mom, my sister, and me. My goatee was rocking. Don't hate.

Here I am about to go on Fox News to talk to one of my best friends, Kennedy, on her show. I was in Austin, but she was in New York.

My band, The Raging Idiots, onstage with Lindsay Ell.

On the air during my show with my producer Ray at my side. Ray is one of the hardest-working guys I've ever met, and he first started with me as an "illegal" intern. He wasn't getting paid and didn't even get school credit, but he still showed up every day. For a year.

Eddie and me before a Raging Idiots show. We have no preshow routine. Someone basically just yells, "YOU'RE ON!"

With Amy, my cohost and one of my best friends in life. She is one of the greatest humans and makes a pretty good *Price Is Right* model in this photo.

Freaking Garth Brooks came in and sang whatever I wanted. Then he gave me his guitar. I don't geek out much anymore, but it was the GOAT! Greatest of all time!

Seriously. I love my dog, and he loves me. And I loved *Home Alone* 1 and 2, but why did they make 3?

Luke Bryan.
Good dude. Great
musician. Fantastic
performer. I wish I
could say something
bad about him. Let
me think . . . Nope,
I still can't.

Carrie Underwood.
I mean, that's an
iPhone pic and she
still looks perfect.
She's been a great
friend to the show
and to my band The
Raging Idiots.

My town put up this sign. It was one of the coolest moments of my life.

The great thing about radio is that you can, for the most part, wear whatever you want. Even stupid-looking tank tops.

7

FIGHT. GRIND. REPEAT. AND SOMETIMES LOSE

If I had to describe my life in Austin in three words, it would be these: Fight. Grind. Repeat.

When I started doing mornings, soon after I arrived in Texas, and had to start waking up at an ungodly hour, I became very disciplined. I mean, I was never a slacker. In college I hardly had time to breathe. But this was different. The stakes were much higher and the margin for error much smaller. Like I've said before, the first step, foundation—whatever you want to call it— for success is being reliable and on time.

I wanted more than anything to be successful at my job, so I began a routine that I follow to this day:

Wake up at 3 A.M.
Arrive at the office by 4 A.M.

Start the show at 5 A.M.

Lunch at 10:30 A.M.

Nap before noon (if it's not before noon, I don't take a nap)

Work out at 3 P.M.

In bed by 8 P.M.

If that schedule sounds tough, that's because it is. And remember, I don't drink coffee. But I forced myself to do the right thing over and over and over again until it became ingrained in me. Every day was a fight—a fight against my own exhaustion and a fight against every other show on the air. The chip on my shoulder that I seem to have been born with only made me that much more competitive. If everyone else in radio was out to get me, I was going to retaliate by getting every listener out there on my side. Fighting every day—that was the grind. And then I just woke up again at 3 A.M. to repeat it.

My fight club mentality was good for the show but not quite as great for my personal life. There was a period in Austin of about five years that I was single. That's one hell of a dry spell to have in your twenties. It got so bad that it became a running joke on the air; we kept a tally of how long it had been since I'd had sex. That's right, I didn't have sex. Not one time. In five years.

I liked to say that my hours were not conducive to a social life. Not too many girls love going to dinner at four thirty in the afternoon. But the truth is that my problem with women ran much deeper than having to ask them out for an early-bird special.

It started with an inherent sense of guilt that makes casual sex impossible for me. I have a similar viewpoint on food, sex, and anything else that is pleasurable but could potentially affect my life in a negative way. Before I engage in the act, I always ask myself, Is it worth the risk? Is it worth the worry about the potential risk? Then I weigh the rewards against the punishment.

For example, if I drink a milk shake, I'll enjoy that milk shake for twenty minutes. But then I'm going to feel guilty about it for about five hours. When I compare those two time periods, there is no question about what I'm going to do: skip the milk shake.

It's the same thing with sex. If I have sex with someone, it'll be great for an hour or two—or seven minutes. But then what happens if I get the girl pregnant, or I get a disease? What if I mess with her head or lie to her? What if she falls in love with me and I can't commit? What if I fall in love with her and she wants nothing to do with me? Seven minutes of pleasure has the potential to be followed up by a day, week, month, or eighteen years of difficulty, discomfort, or even pain. Pure logic dictates what the best decision is for me. I avoid.

I was always able to think with a clear head (sometimes too clear a head). So I didn't have sex with a woman unless she was my girlfriend. But here's where we get to my second problem—I don't have many girlfriends (I've only had five in my entire life), because I'm as terrified of emotional intimacy as I am of getting gonorrhea.

It's hard to be with me if you're a girl. I'm awful, but not in the way a lot of guys are. I'm not the type who doesn't call or leaves dirty clothes all over the place. I try to do great things for the women I do get a chance to date. I enjoy doing big, elaborate, thought-out, romantic gestures. You know, the it-obviously-took-me-a-month-to-put-this-together kind of thing.

During my first Valentine's Day in Austin I was just so excited that I had a girlfriend, I went all out. I had started dating Wilma

Flintstone (not her real name) soon after I moved to Texas (it was after her that I began my five-year stint as a celibate monk). A couple of years younger than me and really cute, she was an intern at the radio station when I was doing my show at night. Soon we started dating. It wasn't super serious, but it was nice. So Valentine's Day rolled around and I was raring to go. I went over to her apartment and immediately presented her with an iPod. "Oh, you got me an iPod," she said. "That's so sweet." Hug. Hug. Kiss. Kiss.

She didn't yet know that I had not only bought her an iPod but also fully loaded it with all her favorite music. But lest you think that was my big romantic gesture, I was just getting started.

"Oh, I've got to go out to the car real quick," I said. "Hey, listen to Song 7."

Why Song 7, you ask?

Well, in the middle of Wilma's medley of favorite indie rock music it cut off and suddenly my voice came through the iPod.

"Go ahead and lock the door and come outside," the recording of my voice went.

Wilma did just as the iPod told her to; she locked the door and went outside, where she was greeted by a trail of flowers, made to look like arrows, leading her down the stairs and straight to a huge limo I had rented. I had even put my clothes in the limo so I could make a quick change before she got down to the car. I felt like I was Carrie Underwood doing a wardrobe change during a concert as I peeled off my sweats and T-shirt and jumped into a pair of slacks and a button-up. (Although I struggled with the tie, so it wasn't fully tied when she arrived at the car, which would have never happened to Carrie. Of course, she has dressers.)

When I plan this kind of massive display of emotion, I am

the best boyfriend. But really I'm the worst boyfriend, because I'm not good at proving emotion through words. I can romance like crazy, but I can't say those three little words: "I love you." And because of that, no act, no matter how romantic, can ever be enough.

Wilma and I reached the inevitable I-love-you impasse the following Christmas. Because I had never said those words, and she was understandably nervous to be the first one to say them, she decided to illustrate them instead.

After finishing a pre-Christmas dinner out and returning to my apartment, both of us prepared for our gift exchange. I don't remember exactly what I got her—probably a journal with the time and date of every single time we had made eye contact or one of my classics, *The Book of Us*.

Of all the things my friends have made fun of me for, *The Book of Us* may be the winner-winner-chicken-dinner of them all. It is exactly what it sounds like; it's a book that celebrates all the memories I've shared with a woman. This is no small thrown-together book. It's memories of first dates, menus from wonderful meals, notes written after really great times together, movie ticket stubs, hair left in the sink (just kidding about the hair. Or am I?). I did the ol' *Book of Us* twice, once for Wilma. I honestly can't remember if it was for this exact Christmas. But you get the point; I gave her the gift I had been working on for months.

Then she handed me my gift, which I quickly unwrapped. As soon as I saw it, though, I wished I had taken a lot longer. It was a picture of the two of us together in a frame covered in the words "I love you," in seven different languages!

I freaked out so badly that I couldn't even remember how to speak English.

"Whoa, whoa, whoa, whoa, whoa," I said in a repeat loop as I laid the frame down and backed away from it like it was an explosive device.

With tears welling up in her eyes, she said, "I just want you to know that I do love you, and this was the easiest way."

You want to know the worst thing in the world? It's when someone says "I love you" and you don't say it back.

I obviously said what I was supposed to say—in that I said, "That's awesome." And then I followed it up with a hug. And then a kiss. I figured that if my mouth was busy, that was a good way of getting out of what I knew she wanted to hear. It was truly out of one of those Southwest Airlines "Wanna Get Away" commercials. Wilma wasn't fooled by my plan, and the fact that I didn't say "I love you" to her became a thing. Not that it hadn't already been a thing between us, but for the rest of our one and a half years of dating, it seemed to consume every other aspect of our relationship. It became the *only* thing.

There was nothing wrong with Wilma. The problem was 100 percent with me. I should have said I loved her. But as soon as a girl got too close, I started to withdraw. When we would get together, I was quiet and closed off. I would go away for periods of time. I put up all kinds of walls.

Love from another human being made me scared, mainly because I was afraid to return it. I have a real vulnerability issue. It doesn't make sense, since by not reciprocating I pushed women away, but I worried about the power someone else would have over me if I gave her my love. Once you put it all out there, you no longer have any control. The other person may leave anyway, and I'll be crushed by the fact that my love wasn't enough for them to stay. I'm only safe whenever it feels like it's not real. Like when

I'm doing my radio show and I can't see the faces of my listeners. Then I'm safe. But when it comes to one-on-one relationships— romantic or with friends—I'm just not able to fully go there. I know it stems from my messed-up childhood, and I'm sure some- one could write a great country song about it. I watched my dad bail out and had a mom who was there physically, but not always there emotionally. I really didn't stand much of a chance, I guess. And I knew I wasn't going to get over it on my own.

I, of course, didn't come to all this stuff on my own. When I signed my contract in Austin, it wasn't only the first time I had a morning show but also the first time I had health benefits. Get- ting insurance was such a big deal to me, because I never had it before, that I actually read the brochure that HR gives you from the health insurance company explaining the benefits available to me. One of the things I saw was that I could go to therapy.

I was definitely interested in the idea of going to talk to some- one but also embarrassed. I'd never talked to anyone. Not like that, not on any really deep level. It just wasn't how I grew up. My mom and I never had a talk about the real stuff of life. Ever. Not once. I don't know that we ever had a real conversation that involved advice or feelings. My grandmother was there for me, but even with her there was such an age gap between us that her perspective seemed about as helpful as if Abe Lincoln were laying some wisdom down. Eloquent, but not too helpful. (That being said, my grandma did teach me how to two-step. It was embarrassing learning how to "dance like they do at the VFW" with my grandma on the kitchen floor. But to her credit, I've been able to use that dance to my advantage many times over the years. Thanks, Grandma!)

If I were ever going to learn how to communicate like a normal, healthy adult, I would definitely need professional help. I went through a few different therapists, and none of them felt right. I read on the Internet that this was normal. (The Internet is my source for finding everything from directions to restaurants to dates to mental health practitioners.) When I finally met a therapist I really bonded with, it was life changing.

I just fell in love with therapy. Linda, my therapist, didn't care—and I say that in the best way possible. Without a vested interest in my life, she offered an impartial perspective. I never had that before. I had people who felt sorry for me or people who wanted me to succeed. To have someone with no agenda and a lot of training in how to find meaning through words and just listen to me was a total eye-opener. I realized I didn't need her to tell me what my faults were. By just sitting and listening to myself talk, I learned enough about myself that I could tick them off one by one. In her office I went to places I never thought of before. I parsed out my desires from my fears, assumptions from realities, and strengths from weaknesses.

In the five years during which I saw Linda, I made sense of all my issues. They didn't go away, but I gathered some tools and understanding so I could at least try to work through my fears of getting close to another human being. For that I have to give a shout-out to my therapist. We talked for hours and hours about that subject alone. You know what, she should give me a shout-out, since those sessions were still seventy bucks an hour with insurance. I know you're reading this, Linda. When you do your therapy book, throw my name in the acknowledgments!

As I said, there's no magic bullet in therapy, and despite the good, hard work I did in that seat across from Linda, I was still not Mr. Open when, years later, I met my next girlfriend, Betty

Boop (not her real name). I grew more when I was with her than with any other person, but even at my most emotionally available, I'm not emotionally available.

Oddly enough, I met Betty while I was on a date with another girl in 2008. She was at a bar with a group of friends, and the girl I was on a date with had some friends in that same group. Betty and I didn't exchange numbers or anything. But in a stroke of fate, I saw her again a week later, on Halloween night, and got her number then. The other girl and I hadn't worked out, as with most girls I go out with. (I have a lot of "one and dones" in my dating life, and they all follow a similar narrative. I'll be out in a bar with my buddies, and since I don't drink, I just hang out, dance, and talk to any female who will listen to me. As the night goes on, people get drunker. As girls get drunker, they like me more. So more than a few times, I've ended up dancing, making out, and getting a hot girl's number, only to have her not remember me the next day. At all. Still, she'd usually feel guilty enough to go on one date, and then . . . she'd be done.)

From my first date with Betty, I knew things with her would be very different and that we were going to date for a long time. We just clicked, whatever that means. Betty, who had just moved to town to take a sales job, had no idea I was on the radio. That was really appealing to me, because I could never lose that sense of mistrust that anyone who knew I had achieved a modicum of success would never like me for me. She had such a positive vibe. We had a fantastic time. It didn't matter what we did or where we went, it was just fun to be with her. We both smiled a lot that night and for many nights after.

During our first night out together, Betty mentioned that she loved Tabasco sauce. I like to listen to people. That's why I'm good at interviewing people and at doing nice things for people in my life. By listening closely, I discover the little things that are important to others. There is nothing that makes someone feel more special than remembering something small and seemingly inconsequential that they said—and I like to make people feel special.

Knowing we were going out again the next week, I rush-ordered a huge bottle of Tabasco sauce that was so big it looked like a wine bottle. Then I went and bought a wooden box made to hold a bottle of wine and had her name carved into it. When I went to pick her up, I handed her the box and said, "I really had a great time on our first date, so I wanted to give you this."

She took the box, which she clearly thought was a bottle of wine, and gave me the kind of "Oh, thanks" you do when someone's done something kind of sweet. But when she opened it up and saw the big bottle of Tabasco sauce, she was *really* happy. Nailed it!

It was nice to have someone to make feel special. Being with Betty, though, I discovered something new in the kind of comfort that only a person who cares about you can provide. Betty was supportive and nurturing of me in so many ways, but I knew she was a real find after I had my wisdom teeth out.

Now, I know what you're thinking: You had your wisdom teeth pulled? It's not like you had your leg amputated. Well, sometimes I wish I had. See, my wisdom teeth were so impacted they had grown back into my jawbone. That's what you get when you never go to the dentist as a kid. (It took me seven or eight years to catch up with my dental work enough that now, my teeth, some of which are fake and some of which aren't, are great.)

In order to take out my wisdom teeth, they had to break my

jaw, which was crazy. I was petrified, not just of the pain but also of not being able to speak, because that's my livelihood. I wasn't in a place yet where I could coast; I had to keep working, which meant keep talking.

To this day, I'm terrified of losing my voice. I think that's why I'm such a germophobe. I'm afraid that if I get sick, it's going to take me off the air. If it takes me off the air, I'm going to get fired. If I get fired, I'm going to be back home. It's why I don't like touching hands or doorknobs. I don't want to lose my job.

The recovery from this dental surgery was months. I could talk, but it was one of the most miserable experiences I've ever had. I wouldn't take any medicine because I wanted to be mentally there while I was on the radio. The pain grew almost unbearable when I developed dry socket, which is basically as bad as it gets. That's when the blood clot that forms in the socket after a tooth has been pulled dissolves, and the bone and nerves it was protecting are now completely exposed. The dentist put gauze in it. As I said, almost unbearable.

Meanwhile I had to spend four hours a day talking—and not just regular talk, but loud, funny, thoughtful, and engaging talk. It was a nightmare. I don't know how I did it and didn't lose every listener I'd fought so hard to get. I just gutted my way through it every day at work. Then I went home and fell into bed, where I stayed for the rest of the day and night.

During those months where I had to go to the dentist almost every day Betty took care of me like crazy. She was there every day, somehow managing to do her job and be my nurse. In the beginning, when I was really sick and couldn't do anything, she took me to the bathroom, mushed up my food, and put warm washcloths on my head as if we'd been married for thirty years.

Betty's nursing me back to health while I recovered from a couple of teeth getting pulled was nothing, though, compared to how she supported me when my mom died. As soon as she heard the news, Betty left work and was by my side, which she refused to leave. Even when I begged her not to come to the funeral, she just shook her head. "There's no way," she said. "I'm going to be there even if I drive in a car behind you."

Betty was right not to listen to me—about anything—since I had been in shock ever since I got the news about my mom's passing the morning of October 21, 2011. It was 8:45 A.M., right in the middle of the Friday Morning Dance Party.

I knew immediately something was wrong when I saw that my sister was calling me while I was on air. No one who knows me calls during the show, because they know I'd never answer the phone. But as soon as I saw my sister's number pop up on my phone, I hit a song and answered it. This was so out of character for me that, deep down, I must have already understood my mother was gone.

When I picked up the phone, sure enough, my sister Amanda was crying. "Mom's dead," she said.

"What happened?" I asked.

"They found her in the kitchen."

That didn't answer my question, but I knew what had happened to our mom. Just a few days earlier Amanda and I had talked about trying again to get her into rehab.

"I'll call you after the show," I said.

Lunchbox and Amy were looking at me, so I quickly explained that my mom had died. Then the song ended and, boom, we were back on the air. Amy started crying so hard that I had to turn her mic off. It was strange for me to see her so upset, because her reaction should have been mine. She was feeling the pain that I should have been feeling. I should have been crying like that. But I wasn't.

Instead, I focused on the remaining hour and fifteen minutes of the show. I couldn't just leave. What was I going to do in that hour that I couldn't do later? Nothing. I have no idea what I talked about that day, but I just kept talking and finished the show without any of my listeners knowing anything was wrong.

Like many children of alcoholics, I'm incredible at compartmentalizing my emotions. Yeah, my mom had just died, but I had a radio show to do, so as everyone else around me cried, I pushed the news to the side. It didn't exist for me.

As soon as the show was over, though, I jumped into high gear and dealt with all the business around my mother's death. I got the basic information, flew home, made the funeral arrangements, paid for them—all without any feeling of loss whatsoever.

It wasn't until three days after she died, while I was speaking at the funeral, that I finally felt the full weight of grief. The hardest thing I've ever done was give my mom's eulogy. I was crying so hard in front of everyone—including Betty, my sister and her two kids, my mom's sisters and their families (my uncle Bub had already died from his demons)—that I didn't think I was actually going to get through it. If it weren't for someone's phone going off with "Bad, Bad Leroy Brown" as its ringtone, I definitely wouldn't have made it. But when I heard Jim Croce singing, "Bad, bad Leroy Brown, the baddest man in the whole damned town," I couldn't help but feel it was a sign from my mom.

A large part of my grief came from the fact that her dying meant the end of my dream that I could become successful enough to make things right with my mother. My story is the

BOBBY BONES

story of pretty much anyone close to somebody with an addiction. I would have loved to solve my mother's problems for her no matter how much time, money, or heartbreak it caused me. It just wasn't possible.

Once I began to make money in radio I was happy to spend it on her, naively believing that if I could make her life easier maybe she wouldn't have to resort to drowning herself in alcohol or drugs. Still, I was wary for obvious reasons whenever she asked me for money. When she told me she couldn't make the rent payments on the piece of land where her trailer sat, I decided to buy it for her. I saved up seven thousand dollars and purchased the two acres of land right outside of Mountain Pine, so that she wouldn't have that excuse anymore.

But like anyone who tries to help an addict in this way, I learned that there were always more excuses. It wasn't the land anymore. It was the trailer payment. When it wasn't the trailer, it was the electric bill. She might have owed money, but the real culprit behind her problems was the evil influence of drugs and alcohol in her life.

A couple of years before she died, I went back to her trailer outside of Mountain Pine to visit her (she never came to visit me in Austin) and found her passed out on the couch with an empty bottle of mouthwash right next to her. She was drunk on mouthwash because she couldn't afford booze. That was a terrible moment for me. I was faced with the reality of how low my mom had fallen, and saw with stark clarity that her life was consumed by drinking. She had to be intoxicated to survive.

The way she lived took a toll on her appearance as the years went by. Her face was worn down and her teeth were those of someone who's been a lifelong addict or never brushed her teeth.

Or both. She put her body through hell, so that although she was still small and thin, she now had a bloated gut. When my mother died, she was forty-seven years old, but she had the body of someone much, much, much older because of all the abuse it had endured.

My mother's problems grew progressively worse in the year leading up to her death. My friend Scotty—our next-door neighbor from when we lived in my stepdad Keith's house and the only friend from home who I am still connected to—drove with me up to her trailer during one of my visits to Mountain Pine. There we found her passed out on the ice, her truck door wide open. There's no question she would have died if we hadn't driven there that day. We picked her up and carried her inside to call the ambulance, and I could tell Scotty was embarrassed for me.

Scotty didn't know the half of it. Dragging my mother, who has passed out in the ice and snow, back into her trailer was a picnic compared to the lowest moment imaginable. Right before she died, my mom called me for the reason she always called me: to ask for money. She was in a bad place, and I didn't want to give it to her. Money was my only bargaining chip. I knew she wasn't going to be homeless because I had bought her land and her trailer, so I didn't have to worry that she'd be out on the streets. Well, she gave me something else to worry about.

"If you don't give it to me," she said, "I'm going to put out a tape of me having sex on the Internet."

I forget how much money she wanted—maybe five hundred dollars. The amount is irrelevant. I didn't hear anything more after my mother extorted money from me by threatening to put out a porno. I just gave her the money.

I was angry with her for so many things. I was angry about

all the times I tried to get her help and she refused it. There were so many times we sat and talked about how she needed help. Or rather, I talked.

"Let me do this for you."

"Don't you want to get better?"

Her response to whatever argument I made was to say whatever it took to end the conversation. And that's what happened many, many, many times. Even if somehow she did agree to go to rehab, it was never for long.

I was mad, I was sad, I was confused, I felt sorry for her, and I loved her—all at once, and I had no idea what to do.

I was also angry with her for my genetic tendency toward addiction, which, even if I didn't have my mother's glaring example to remind me anymore, was always there lurking in the shadows of my own behavior. Alcohol wasn't my source of obsession, but almost everything else was or could be. Hobbies that for most people were harmless easily became a fixation for me. That's what happened when I began playing poker a couple of years after I moved to Austin.

My grandma taught me how to gamble when I was five years old; I learned the value of every card and the rules around odds. Recognizing that I was pretty good with numbers, Grandma taught me everything I knew. Once I had some money to spare, though, the rush of winning and losing took cards to a whole new level.

A couple of times a month, Lunchbox and I would go to Las Vegas, where I'd play in massive poker tournaments that lasted upwards of thirteen hours. That was just the start. I played online all the time as well as in a ton of underground games. The problem wasn't money. I actually made a decent amount playing poker. (Once I even won a Las Vegas tournament with a pot of over fifteen thousand dollars.)

The problem was that for several years all that I did besides work was play poker, read about poker, or practice poker math scenarios. That was my life. I didn't realize how deep I was until one day I looked at my bookshelf, and every book on it was about poker, or odds, or Doyle Brunson, or other famous players. I thought to myself, Okay. I've reached a point in my life where this is all that I'm doing. This is more than a hobby; I am addicted to playing poker. And like that, I quit. Just stopped and didn't play anymore.

The same thing happened with golf. (I could shoot in the low eighties at my best, starting with an average score of over 110 only a couple of years earlier.) I got decent at the impossible sport not because I'm a natural athlete but because I would go and practice for four hours a day, five, six days a week. Just like with poker, that's all I did. And again, just like with poker, I had to quit because I became too obsessed. I haven't touched a club aside from a charity tournament a couple of times a year (where I tell myself I'm not really "playing"). I could tell the same story over and over again. It didn't matter if it was poker, golf, work, exercise, diet: I only seem to be able to do things in extremes. Just like my mom.

I came to understand a lot of this in therapy, where I also learned about enabling the addict. In the case of my mom, I would have done anything if it meant she would get sober. At first it was buying her a couple of acres. Then it was buying her a place to live. I naively thought money would make her life easier so she could focus on other things—like her compulsion to get drunk. But that's not what happened.

It didn't matter what I did: my mother was not going to stop drinking just because I wanted her to. Everyone around the addict can want whatever they want, but until the addicted person actually wants to get sober, nothing is going to change. My mom was never committed to changing. I don't think she even contemplated it.

When I was crying at my mom's funeral, I don't know what I was really mourning—her death, or my dream of saving her.

Ironically, though, it wasn't until after my mom died that I had my most personal moment with her. When my sister was clearing out the trailer, she found a note my mom had written to me but had never sent. In it, she talked about when I guest-hosted *Live with Regis and Kelly*. Now, at the actual time that I hosted the morning show with Kelly Ripa, in early 2011, my mom didn't have any kind of reaction. None. For all I knew, it wasn't a big deal to her. (To me it was a huge deal.) It was like the rest of my career: my mom never really seemed to care that much.

But apparently she watched me when I was on TV with Kelly Ripa, where I played a funny song I wrote called "I Want My Mom to See Me on TV."

It was the first time she really kind of understood what I did—and she was touched by it. "I loved when you played that song on TV," she wrote, "because I felt like you were talking to me."

BONES GOES COUNTRY

I was scared to death as I drove up to Truluck's restaurant. It was 2011. No, I wasn't taking Kate Beckinsale out for dinner. (Although, Kate, I'm still available . . .) I was at the fancy seafood and steak house in North Austin to meet Rod Phillips, an executive at Clear Channel, the humongous radio company that now owned my radio show.

I was intimidated because Rod was the first executive I'd ever met. A national guy who had overseen the programming for regional markets that stretched from Miami to Chicago to Waco to what seemed like Egypt, the SVP of programming was known for his ability to make stations and the on-air "talent" better.

Getting a visit from corporate was kind of like being called to the principal's office, even though there was really nothing for me to be nervous about. Over the last eight years, I had built

The Bobby Bones Show into a decent radio program with a few affiliates scattered around the country. My tiny syndication company began back in 2005 when I begged the manager of KZCH in Wichita, Kansas, to put our show on his station. I literally begged. And pleaded. And maybe cried. And offered to do it for free! (I actually went into the hole with the Wichita deal, but it was worth it in the end.) Wichita didn't have a morning show, and the station manager knew my old champion and local station manager Jay Shannon, so I (and Jay) asked him if he'd take a chance on me and a new technology called Comrex, which allowed us to transmit the show through the Internet. These days Comrex works seamlessly, but back then it was awful. It died three or four times a show, so that we had to reset it constantly. But we made it work, and eventually we won in Wichita.

(As soon as we became the number one morning show in Wichita, I said on air, "I will always be loyal to you guys." And I have been. I go back to Wichita every year. Now we're on The Bull, the country station there, and we've been number one there forever. When my band the Raging Idiots announced a show date at Wichita's Orpheum Theater in the fall of 2015, we had to add another because the first sold out in less than forty minutes—faster than any other in the Orpheum's ninety-two-year history. Yeah, literally outsold the Avett Brothers, Ray Charles, and Glen Campbell's farewell tour. That was pretty cool. Sorry if that sounds braggy.)

I'm indebted to Wichita because it was there that we proved we could win in a place besides Austin, and after Wichita we were able to get bigger syndication deals in both Amarillo and Lubbock, Texas. And that's when Rod Phillips arrived on the scene. Rod didn't turn out to be the "corporate guy" I thought he was at all. He was just an ordinary dude in jeans, a polo shirt, and three-day stubble.

"You know, we're messing up by not using you," he said over his steak and what I was having because of whatever weird diet I was on at the time. It could have been fish with no butter; or an extra large slab of beef with extra butter to put on weight; or a veggie plate, as I also had my vegetarian chapter.

"I want to put you on a couple of my stations," Rod said, "because I think you're good enough to do that."

I couldn't believe someone outside my building was telling me I was good. For years I had been hearing Jay Shannon telling me I was good. But he was my station manager. Your own program director or station manager is always supposed to tell you you're good—otherwise why would he have hired you in the first place? Rod, on the other hand, was the first guy on a broader level to like what I was doing and then fly all the way to Austin to tell me.

Even better than the compliments, he started putting my show on affiliates inside the company. He put *The Bobby Bones Show* on in Tuscaloosa, Alabama. Then it was Albany, Georgia. Soon, all in all we were on in more than thirty cities because Rod championed the show on a national level.

In the summer of 2012, Rod and I started talking about the idea of me putting my show on some country stations. Having grown up in Arkansas, I had country music in my blood. In fact, I got in trouble many times for putting country acts on my Top 40 show. I never worried too much about labels. It was just about finding the best music or best talent out there. Eli Young Band, Pat Green, Dierks Bentley, and Willie Nelson all came on when I was on pop radio. And man, did I get crushed by my Top 40 music directors for putting on "country and western acts."

(Side note: it's so weird how things change but stay the same. Now I am constantly scolded for putting acts on our show that aren't "country" enough. So, like in real life, I never really fit in perfectly on the radio, either. I may be the only guy to play 2Pac into Luke Bryan into Lou Bega on a country station. I also bring in acts to perform on the country stations that aren't country at all. I've had Ed Sheeran in performing live. Even Shaggy came in to do a couple of songs. Yeah, "It Wasn't Me" Shaggy. The station managers were like "WTF?")

Because Rod and I had been talking about my moving into a country format, I didn't think it was all that odd when he invited me to the Country Music Awards in November. "I know you're wanting to spread the word about your show," Rod said. "So why don't you come to Nashville? Everyone's going to be in town at the same time. Station managers, company managers. Ordinarily it'd be tough to get all these people in the same room."

He didn't have to ask twice. I booked my Southwest flight and off I went to do my Top 40 show from the heart of country music, and hopefully get station managers to see it was a good fit for their stations. Almost as soon as I landed in Nashville, Rod and his team (from the company then known as Clear Channel but later rebranded iHeartMedia) were wining and dining me. Well, just dining me. They took me to so many awesome dinners and cool places it was freaky. Maybe they just like me, I thought to myself. But that wasn't what it turned out to be at all.

On my second day in Nashville, Rod casually suggested we check out a shoot where all these top bands were doing national promos for our company. "Of course!" was my speedy reply. Tim McGraw was there; Lady Antebellum was there; Carrie Underwood was there. And everyone was super nice, and so clearly

A-game. "Well, this is pretty cool," I thought to myself. "I'm in Nashville to meet all of the bosses. And I get to see a few country stars, too!"

Right after I got done talking SEC football with Tim McGraw (and texting all of my friends, "I've been talking with Tim McGraw for the last twenty minutes about college football!"), Rod took me aside and gave me one of those serious the-police-are-outside-to-take-you-to-jail looks. "Listen," he said. "You're about to be hammered. They're going to tell you something that will really shake you up. I shouldn't even be telling you this, but I just wanted to give you a warning, so brace yourself."

What?

Thanks, Rod Phillips! I mean, what the heck did that mean? Was I about to get fired? You brought me out here to fire me? I imagined the worst flight home ever: being fired and then having to sit on a plane for two hours wondering why. I know it's not customary for bosses to take their employees out to big fancy dinners and promo shoots if they are about to fire them, but common sense wasn't floating around anywhere in my head in that moment.

It only got worse when I was taken over to a corner of the video shoot where huddled together was a group of bigwigs: Rod; John Ivey, the program director of KIIS FM in Los Angeles, one of the two biggest Top 40 stations in America; and Clay Hunnicutt, who was then the director of country for Clear Channel, were gathered around talking. They sat me down and said, "We want you to move to Nashville to be our national country morning show."

And then I went deaf. Just like when something loud pops in your ears, I heard a loud *beeeeeeep* and then nothing after that.

I was shocked. Their offer came out of nowhere for me. It was the last thing I was expecting. I really thought I was going to Nashville to *pitch* my Top 40 show, based in Austin, to any station manager who would listen—not to be asked if I wanted to broadcast the largest daily country morning show in the history of the format across tons of Clear Channel's markets.

"Are you kidding?" was all I could manage to say. They took a picture of me as they asked me the question. In the photo, I'm pink haired (it was Breast Cancer Awareness Month) and my jaw was on the ground. I was shocked, sad, and slightly excited at the same time. In that order.

I didn't say yes right away, not only because I was in shock but also because I really didn't know how to feel about the offer. On the career side of things, I had built this entire "empire" in the pop format. It was a small empire, but it was definitely expanding. I had already accepted the fact that I wasn't going to get a morning spot on Top 40 stations in New York or L.A. Elvis Duran and Ryan Seacrest had both just signed new contracts, and they weren't going anywhere anytime soon. They were giants. But I was content in continuing to grow from where I was. In addition to my regular morning gig, I had started cohosting a new national sports show on Fox Sports Radio with tennis champ Andy Roddick. (Let me sidebar on Andy, who in addition to having become one of my best friends is also one of the most obnoxious and best humans in the entire world. That dude can be a real dick on the tennis court or golf course. But man, he is a quality human being. One of the best people I've ever met.)

Despite the fact that I was comfortable with what I had done in Austin, I wasn't stupid. I recognized that there was much more room for me to grow inside of country—the biggest format in America and one in which I felt comfortable because of my background and my deep appreciation for the music. But there was one other major factor that kept me from jumping at the promotion: I loved Austin. I mean I really loved Austin.

I was supposed to hate it, because I'm from Arkansas, and when you grow up in Arkansas, you are taught to hate Texas. Texas is the bigger and better brother—particularly when it comes to sports. So as an Arkansas sports fan, I was pretty wary when I first moved to Austin. But the people there are so great. The city embraced us, which was particularly unbelievable for as cool a place as Austin to do to a small gang of—well—idiots, who had never done a morning show like ours. In a city where everyone is always trying to be the biggest hipster in the room, my approach was always to keep it real. I mean I-hang-out-at-Chili's-and-shop-at-Walmart real. And people loved us for it. I couldn't imagine anything better.

I thanked the Clear Channel execs, who expected me to answer "yes" right away, and immediately went back to my hotel room, where I called Betty.

"You're not going to believe what just happened," I said to her. "I was just offered a national show from Nashville. They want me to move here and be the national country guy."

I know that it had to be hard for her to hear, because the offer meant I would have to move away. I already wasn't the easiest boyfriend in the world; a long-distance relationship would only make things more difficult. Still, because she cared about me so much, her immediate reaction was to think only of me.

"You have to do it," she said.

It's crazy just how supportive and unselfish she was. I don't have that inside of me. But she did. She didn't need to think about it. In a beat, her response was "You have to take the job."

I was scared—not to go to country, because that was awesome. And not to go to Nashville, because Nashville's awesome. It was because I had to kick down everything I had spent the last seven years building from the ground up and start all over. It felt very much like the move from Little Rock to Austin. I'd never been there before, but I had to do it.

"You're right," I said to Betty. "I have to do it."

A few days later, I told the execs at Clear Channel that my answer was yes.

Of course, it wasn't quite as simple as that. These kinds of offers are always followed by a lot of negotiating on both sides. One thing that wasn't up for negotiation, however, was the rest of my crew on *The Bobby Bones Show*. I wasn't coming unless all of the team could come too. If they wanted the show, well, Amy, Lunchbox, Ray, Eddie, and the rest of my crew *were* the show. Thankfully, that wasn't a sticking point.

Even though the gang had new jobs in Nashville if they wanted them, they still couldn't know for a long time, which was weird for me. It went from uncomfortable to problematic when Amy and her husband picked a house to buy in Austin. Luckily (for me), something happened and the deal on the house fell through. But I went to Rod and said, "If we don't tell Amy now, she's going to buy another house." So I got special dispensation to tell her months before everyone else. She was in immediately. Because for Amy, the bigger her platform, the more good she can do in the world. Also, despite how much the rest of us drive her nuts, she still likes being part of the gang. Crazy girl.

Eventually I was able to call in each person on the show one by one and tell them that I had some information I needed to share, but I had to have them sign a nondisclosure agreement first—which scared everyone. As soon as they had put pen to paper, I told them the news quickly. I didn't take any pleasure from torturing people.

Except Lunchbox. He was the only person I messed with.

"There's going to be a lot of changes," I said.

"What kind of changes?" he asked nervously.

"The changes involve you."

"Okay."

"It's tough for me to tell you this . . ."

I dragged it out forever. I took many deep breaths. I even faked a half cry. It was an Oscar-worthy performance. I wish I had taped it!

"I'm going to be leaving," I said.

His eyes got real big.

"I'm really sorry that I have to leave. I don't know what you're going to do . . . but I hope you're going to come with me, because they've offered us a national show out of Nashville!"

He didn't know whether to hug me or kill me. It was awesome.

On Monday, February 4, 2013, we formally announced that *The Bobby Bones Show* was moving to Nashville; Friday was our last show in Austin. I know this might not seem like big news to most of you reading this, but it made some waves in the city that built our radio show. As the *Austin Chronicle*'s Abby Johnston wrote about me: "He assembled his own dream team and turned KISS FM's negligible ratings into a national goldmine, far out-scoring any other local show. . . .

"The show feels like a conversation between friends, and that's what kept me listening. I love to hate Lunchbox's antiquated and misogynistic attitude toward women and his party-boy lifestyle. . . . Lunchbox's foil, Amy, has captivated listeners with her struggle to have a child, and as she chokes up on air, I've shed tears with her. . . . Mostly, though, there's Bobby, who through the years has revealed himself as one of the most genuine and open hosts on the radio."

Not everyone was as emotional about our leaving. As someone's comment to a post about our announcement on a local TV news channel's Facebook page shows:

"I'll miss Bobby, but if he's taking Lunchbox with him I'll throw him a party!!"

Lunchbox is an acquired taste.

Jokes aside, it was a monster when we left. That Friday, my last day on the air, I cried like a baby. Lunchbox and Amy each said some final words on the air, and then they left the room, until it was just me. Alone, I just cried and cried. It was my second time sobbing on air. The first was when I had been jumped and feared for my life. This time it was because I had loved the show so much.

We hadn't been the funniest on the radio. But in the land of hip and SXSW, we broke the mold and proved that you don't have to act super cool in a city that is super cool. We talked about stuff like our love of the unlimited salad at Olive Garden. Austin embraced us because we were real humans, and none more so than me. Austin was the place where I grew into adulthood.

Less than a month after I said good-bye to Austin, *The Bobby Bones Show* arrived in Nashville. When we launched, we were in thirty-five country markets with more than two million weekly listeners and set to grow almost immediately to fifty markets nationwide.

The singer-songwriter Chris Janson was our very first guest once we went over to country. I had seen him play for like thirty seconds and thought, Wow, that guy's pretty good. Quite frankly, we needed someone to come and make sure our equipment was good, so I invited him up to play. Our equipment was good and so was Chris.

It was easy for me to slide into the new genre, because as I said, it wasn't all that new to me. The way I talk, the way I act, where I'm from—is country. Even when I was heavy into alternative or hip-hop in my life, I was still always a country music fan.

The only hard part was that everyone who considered himself a real defender of country music hated me. A writer for the alternative weekly *Nashville Scene* summed up the general opinion of me: "I have a hard time seeing how a thirtysomething-year-old Top 40 DJ with no noted background in country music shilling for Clear Channel with a sidekick named 'Lunchbox' is anything to get excited about." Nobody wanted me there. Nobody accepted me. It was just like in junior high and high school, all over again.

Part of the anger toward me was simply change rage. I was taking over for the legendary country DJ Gerry House, who had been on in Nashville forever. He was a very traditional, old-school, inside-the-industry, deep-voiced, cowboy-hat kind of country guy, who had been broadcasting from Nashville for almost forty years when I showed up. I didn't actually replace him; there was a show between his and mine, but it didn't last long. Anytime you follow a great anyone—football coach, CEO, talk show host—it's really hard to succeed. Anyone who comes in after him, it doesn't matter how good they are: they really don't have a chance. And I feel bad for them.

Still, when I got on air, everyone continued to compare me to Gerry—and as much as I respect him, I'm not him. Nothing about me is like him. Not better or worse, just different. But that old chip on my shoulder revealed itself again in the midst of an entire industry saying I was single-handedly going to ruin country music.

In the beginning I might have been a little *too* different. I can admit that now. Deciding I was going to make sure they knew I wasn't coming into their world but that I was just going to bring mine, I blasted hip-hop and pop. I blatantly ignored the "old guard" that is Nashville. And it wasn't just though my musical choices. I also vocally challenged them. I was outspoken with my social views. For example, I went on the air and supported gay rights completely in a format where that's never been accepted. Why should it bother me one bit if two people love each other? Answer: it doesn't. A lot of station managers, however, were not happy about my stance. (That's one thing I haven't changed; I'm a permanent and absolute supporter of gay rights.)

My attitude was "This is how it's going to work. I'm playing whatever I want to play. I'm doing the bits I want to do. I don't wear cowboy boots or hats or belt buckles. I am not you; I am me." Looking back, I wish I hadn't been such a bull in a china shop, so to speak. But live and learn. (By the way, the "old guard" are still not big fans of mine.) It was no wonder that everybody hated my guts.

Well, almost everyone. Not long after I moved to Nashville, Brad Paisley invited me over to his house. With an album to promote, he had been our first Country Top 30 countdown guest, and after that he asked me over as a sort of welcome to Nashville. When I got to his house, he introduced me to his wife, Kimberly Williams. When I talked to her, I couldn't stop thinking, You're talking to the *Father of the Bride* girl. (I know, pretty stupid, but that movie, which she starred in, is a classic.) Then we got on his four-wheeler and drove from the house to the recording studio he has on the property, which is deep in the woods. He showed me the studio and then we walked out onto his property. That's when he said, "People aren't going to like you around here for a long time," he said. "They don't like change. They didn't like me when I started. But I can assure you that if you keep doing what you are doing, they will come around." That meant a lot to me then and still does, years later. He didn't have to do that.

Brad was right—about people not liking me for a long time. From listeners to station managers to the recording industry to the artists, everyone looked at me like the weird radio guy. Nobody wanted me there. It was not pretty. I had the same exact feeling going into work as I had walking into school every day after the T-Bone incident.

Almost a year after we moved to Nashville, I woke up to the fact that my attitude wasn't winning me any friends—or listeners. I needed to get people to like me, or at least feel sorry for me. Working on the theory that it's hard to hate someone if he is getting picked on, I thought, I'm going to turn myself into the one who's getting picked on.

This is the first time I've ever admitted to this story publicly, or privately, for that matter. But here we go. Ready?

What I did was I launched a massive negative PR campaign against myself to garner sympathy. Only one person other than me knew what was going on. My buddy Cruz, a former member of the military who was head of security for the show for a while, was my secret agent as I created a shell company through which to maneuver. I spent about thirteen thousand dollars of my own money to buy billboards all over town.

Then, one beautiful morning in the first week of February 2014, they went up. There were multiple billboards, in the highest-trafficked areas, that said in all-uppercase black letters on a white background, GO AWAY BOBBY BONES. That was it. But that's all it took for people driving around to say either

a. "Why do people want Bobby Bones to go away?"
b. "I agree. Go away, Bobby Bones."

or

c. "Who is Bobby Bones?"

People started talking about it all the time. On the street they would come up to me and say, "Dude, I can't believe people are doing that to you." Then began the speculation on who was crazy enough (and hated me enough) to pay for these expensive billboards. Even news organizations began investigating into the entity behind the signs. Was it a record company? Was it a rival radio station? Was it certain artists who I'd feuded with? (Yes, this has happened.) When media outlets tried to track the original buyer by going to the Nashville outdoor advertising company that had put up the billboards, they were told all that was known about the paying entity: the client who had purchased all four boards for a three-week run was known as "Anti-BOBBY BONES."

Nobody (not even my bosses) thought it was me.

The plan worked. Listeners who were on the fence started to feel sorry for me, because someone had spent all this money to pick on me. And those who had never heard of me before tuned in to hear what a guy who gets billboards telling him to go away had to say. (A year later, when we did market research, people still remembered and remarked on those signs.)

In the middle of all this, the Academy of Country Music announced on February 18 that I had tied with Lon Helton, the longtime host of Westwood One's *Country Countdown USA*, to win the award for National Radio Personality of the Year. The award came out of left field. We hadn't even been on for a full year, and they were giving us the award for being the best? I took to Twitter that day to joke: "I won an ACM for National Radio Personality of the Year today. I'm still waiting for them to 'recall' and recount and take it away."

They didn't recall our award. I had to miss the awards ceremony, because one of my best friends was married the same day. So as Luke Bryan and Blake Shelton hosted and gave out awards, I gave a speech at the wedding of my buddy Ricky, who I call Softball. And I would do it again ten times over. An award is cool, but in the end it's just a dust collector. And I can always hold over Ricky's head that I skipped winning an ACM to be at his wedding, so he can help me move.

The listeners who tuned in out of curiosity after those billboards didn't change the dial, either. *The Bobby Bones Show* grew to nearly seventy affiliates, with about three million weekly listeners, and on the weekends I hosted the *Country Top 30 with Bobby Bones* over more than one hundred affiliate stations.

Now, you may be reading this and thinking that those were pretty desperate measures to take to get more ratings. Under-

handed, even. And I understand that. But you have to understand how hard it was to be rejected for the thing that I had been
doing for years and that had made my radio show so successful—
and that was being myself. When the old-guard country folks
rejected me because I wasn't "country enough," it hurt for lots of
reasons—my background, my respect for the music, but most of
all because I was coming from the same place of authenticity that
I always came from. When I put up the billboards, it was because
I wanted people to take the time to actually listen to the show
and make a judgment on the quality, not a snap judgment based
on the fact that I had previously been on Top 40 radio or on how
I dressed.

When I first came to Nashville, I was unfavorably compared
to Gerry House constantly. It killed me to walk every day into
what used to be his studio and see *his* sign, HOME OF THE HOUSE
FOUNDATION. It was during that period that I said to myself,
"When I hit number one, I'm going to take that sign down."
Until then, I didn't deserve to take it down.

So when we hit number one around a year later, I took a
screwdriver into the studio and removed that sign. I didn't say
anything about it afterward, because I wasn't trying to be disrespectful. I respect anyone who can stay in a job in the entertainment business for any amount of time—particularly one who did
it as well and as long as Gerry. It's not easy, and I know that.

But this was now my workplace, and so I took the two-
by-one-foot sign down. Someone in the building—I don't know
who—called one of the broadcasting trade magazines, which
printed an article about how I was being disrespectful once again.
Another backlash followed, but luckily this time it was just within
the industry. No one outside radio knew or cared about the sign,

which was no surprise to me. Honestly, in the grand scheme of things, Gerry and I, we don't matter much. People move on.

When I took Gerry's sign down, I moved it to the trophy case upstairs, where hopefully my name will go one day. I thought I was doing a natural thing, making my studio my own. But it created discomfort that I didn't want, and I wondered if I hadn't subconsciously made things harder for myself than they needed to be.

While I worked through the tough times at the job, I continued to wreak havoc in my personal life. When it came to women, I sabotaged everything. It was the same old problem over and over. I jeopardized my happiness, because I didn't feel like I deserved it. I worried anyone I committed to would leave me, like everybody else in life had. So in a counterphobic move, I was the one to cut off the relationship every single time.

Betty and I had been dating for more than four years when I arrived in Nashville. When she and I first started to get serious, I'd warned her to stay away from me. Because I cared for her!

"You don't want to be in this relationship," I said, and I meant it.

In the beginning, I tried all my tricks to try to ice her out (not returning texts, bad attitude, going away without telling her). I didn't want to play games or be a jerk. An unconscious fear sabotaged any kind of intimacy in my life. I slowly withdrew without realizing I was doing it. But Betty just stuck with me, and stuck with me. I'm not sure why, because I can't figure out the appeal of dating me.

Four years later, she was still there by my side. When I decided to move to Nashville, she wanted to come with me. But I wasn't having that, of course. I didn't think it was fair to her. Betty was such a great person, it wasn't worth her giving up her whole life to move to a new town for me. She deserved better. She deserved somebody who could love her fully. And it wasn't me. In all those years we were together, I never told her that I loved her.

So Betty stayed in Austin. We tried to make it work for a second. We talked on the phone and she visited, but we both knew that it wasn't going to last. Not long after I moved, we broke up.

I never told her I loved her. And you know what? I probably did. See? I can't even say the words here. In text. In past tense.

Despite the fact that I ran from her like a coward, Betty continued to be a source of support at the times in my life when I needed someone the most. One of those was about a year after we broke up. Out of the blue, I couldn't balance and I couldn't read. I had no clue what had happened, only that it was impossible for me to function on air, and something was really wrong with me. But I didn't tell anybody at work that I was sick, other than Amy, who I needed to cover for me. Again, it was the old paranoia that I'd get fired in a hot second if I showed weakness. I would hand Amy news stories, because I couldn't read them. But sometimes I couldn't even speak in complete sentences. Terrified, I went to the doctor immediately, who didn't put my mind at ease when he said, "This could be a lot of things." There was a lot of "blah blah blah." Then I heard, "You may have MS."

The only neurologist I could get an appointment with quickly was one I found through connections in Austin. So the next day I flew to Austin for an appointment. Worried, I called Betty to explain that I was coming to town and why. She took off from work and met me at the doctor's office, where she stayed in the waiting room for the entire day while I went through a battery of tests including MRIs, CAT scans, and one where I had to do breathing exercises until I passed out with all these weird things attached to my head. No matter how scary the stuff got, it was a relief knowing she was right outside.

It turned out I'd had a seizure in my sleep, and once I knew I wasn't dying, I slowly recovered. It took weeks, but I bounced back fully. The doctor told me that I may suffer from seizures again, but that it isn't anything that I can't handle. My brain is okay, but my mind still has a lot of problems. Case in point—I ran away from Betty because I started to feel things most people really want to feel. As soon as it became apparent this was a girl that I could have a really happy life with, I was out. It didn't take a brain surgeon to know that I had made a huge mistake.

9

GNAWING AT THE BONES

After my breakup with Betty Boop, I was pretty down in the dumps for a while. I went on dates with a few girls, but nothing serious. That is, until the day of "The List."

In case you didn't already pick up on it, I'm a little OCD. So I really like lists. I list the times, places, and locations I need to be every single day. Before the show, I list segments that we are going to do in order of how good I think they will be. After the show, I change that list and list them in order of how well they went on air. I list my favorite soaps. I list my favorite teas. So of course I had a list of pretty girls I wanted to come on my radio show.

Rachel Reinert, one part of the three-member hit country band Gloriana, was definitely on The List. In fact, she might have been at the top of it. When we did a bit on air where we picked the ten most beautiful women in country (given the classy title "The Bones' Babes"), I put Rachel at number one. (*People* magazine had just come out with their "Most Beautiful" issue and didn't pick anyone from the country world, which I found annoying. But the real inspiration behind the segment was my newly single status. As I said on air, "I'm putting a bunch of girls who I would want to date on this list.")

I didn't think it would actually work, of course! But shockingly, it did, because the day after we aired this list, with Rachel on top, her people called up the show and asked if I wanted the singer-songwriter to come to the studio the following day. No way! I thought to myself. How embarrassing. But my rule is, the more embarrassing something is for me, the more the listeners will probably enjoy it. And of course I thought it would be funny to strike out on the air with a beautiful girl who I knew wouldn't want to date me. So I agreed. I even made the whole experience even more embarrassing by writing her a song, which I imaginatively called "Rachel," that I played for her in the studio. It could have won the Grammy for Song of the Year. Here, let me show you:

> *Rachel, I think you are so pretty*
> *When I see you, you make my heart all giddy.*
> *Rachel, I got you that trophy*
> *Do you like guys like me that are dopey?*

She smiled and laughed uncomfortably as I performed the whole thing for her, as if I were a creepy stalker. As you can see, my song stylings have met with varying responses when it comes to the ladies. Luckily, the tunes I cowrite for my band the Raging Idiots get a better reception. But at the end of her visit I got her cell number. Well . . . I had a friend tweet her friend to get me her cell number. I'm a total ladies' man, you know. Anyway, Rachel and I started seeing each other fairly soon after. That's right! She agreed to go out with me. It was very casual at first, as she was on the road a lot and I woke up at 3 A.M. But it turned into a strong relationship.

Rachel was fun to be around. I was just coming off my four-year relationship with Betty, probably the best human I had ever met, and she was a tough act to follow. But going out with Rachel was not only different, but equally good. Betty, who worked in sales, helped me find balance. She was great at that work-life thing, with a successful career *and* a strong circle of friends and close family.

Rachel, who had signed her first publishing deal in her teens and moved to Nashville soon after, was a lot like me—i.e., a workaholic. You have to be if you want to make it in the music business. She was always on the road with Gloriana, which had toured with Taylor Swift and won the Academy of Country Music's award for Top New Vocal Group and a Teen Choice award for Choice Country Group. I would have given her an award, too (oh wait, I did: the Bones' Babes #1 Hottest Country Singer Award). She was one of the greatest singers I've ever heard face-to-face. I would just ask her to play stuff around the house so I could hear her sing. Unfortunately, she never asked me to just tell jokes.

Her talent as a performer was only one aspect of Rachel's appeal. She was also very open-minded in a climate that, in my opinion, can be too judgmental.

Rachel was just cool, but there was never any kind of country music "power couple" thing between us. First of all, I don't go to many industry events because I'm a freaky, antisocial dude who feels like everyone at those parties either wants to use me or doesn't like me. (I know, fun.) I didn't perceive myself as half of any "celebrity relationship," as some gossip sites called us. I also never really thought of Rachel as famous. She was super talented and driven, and I was attracted to that. Yet I also saw the grind of her job from the inside: the long bus rides, the program directors you have to drive all over the country to talk to in order to get your song on the radio, the many, many struggles of being a recording artist.

Struggling, which we all do, whether you're a truck driver or a country music star, is what brought a common humanity not just to Rachel but to all the good and talented folks I've met in Nashville. Recognizing that beneath the makeup, four-hundred-dollar distressed jeans, and perfect hair (or steamed baseball cap—seriously, I've seen some country music dudes get that done to their hats before they go onstage), we're all just the same. Knowing this to be true is what's helped me most with my on-air interviewing of celebrities.

Most people, even those in the media, get intimidated by famous folks. Often interviewers are so worried about making celebrities uncomfortable or unhappy in any way that they ask the same questions as every other journalist, which means the famous person gives the same answer over and over until it becomes muscle memory. I think having to say the same thing again and again is the most annoying thing ever for anyone, famous or anonymous. I'm not in the business of making musicians uncomfortable or annoyed (at least, I don't think I am). So if I can break the verbal rut they're in, there's no telling where I can go. Awful or awesome, either way is great.

The way I do this is by humanizing people who don't seem human to others because of their larger-than-life status. "What did you eat for breakfast?" "Did you have a dog, growing up?" "What kind of underwear do you wear?" I ask about simple stuff that celebrities don't usually get asked.

I do interviews constantly, in a medium where the conventional wisdom is that they're not good for ratings. But I've always felt that listeners tune out when they hear interviews because most people on the radio or television aren't doing interesting interviews. We once were given research that compared *The Bobby Bones Show* to other morning national shows, and what they found was that while other hosts gushed over their guests just for showing up, my interviews were more of a back-and-forth between peers.

I was happy the research bore out what I hope comes through on my show. Not only do I feel the peer-to-peer quality of my questions makes for more interesting radio, but I do believe it also puts the artist at ease. When Blake Shelton and Miranda Lambert split up, I was the first one who got him to talk in any real way about his divorce, because I talked to him in, well, a real way. Instead of asking him a fawning nonquestion, like "It must be so hard for you," or making an accusation, like "Was there someone else?" I went at the angle, "You're famous, and she's famous. And you guys kept it secret until it was finalized. Now, all personal things aside, how did you do that?" With that Blake was able to separate himself a bit, talk about the law, and then he kind of just went, "Our whole thing was, we are going to be cool about this. It is what it is . . . we're buddies." That might not seem like big news to you (and it wasn't to me), but that interview was picked up by every media outlet from the *Today* show to CNN to the *Christian Post*.

Even celebrity listeners, like Tim McGraw, liked what we were doing on the show. Although now we've done a few specials together for TV and radio, the first time he was on our show was when he called in to our request line! The country superstar said he was just a fan of the show and that he listened every day as he drove his kids to school. It was so crazy that honestly we didn't believe it was him, and so we asked him a lot of trivia questions to see if it was really him. (Obviously, he passed with flying colors.) When I moved to Nashville, I had been told, "Tim is really quiet and doesn't warm up quickly to people." But that's not what I found at all. When he found out that I'd never owned or worn a cowboy hat, he gave me the black one he'd worn throughout his whole Las Vegas run. Tim even sent me a murse (man purse) that he had bought but was too embarrassed to wear.

At the beginning, not everyone appreciated my goal to find a shared humanity. When I first started this job, few artists wanted to come on my show because my interview style was so different. A lot of big stars were upset with me because I took them out of their comfort zone. I didn't say, "Hey, let's talk about your record and what inspired this song." Instead I wanted to know what they ate for dinner last night. (That isn't a real question, but rather the kind that always leads to something else. So I ask it, and then I just listen. Often interviewers don't listen to the answers—they are just preparing for their next question. I listen to what the artist is saying, because that's what takes me to my next question.)

Jason Aldean, one of the biggest guys in country music, acted like he hated me when he came on the show. He didn't think my questions were amusing and rarely smiled. Because of that I didn't really like him, either. That's not childish, is it? But now, we totally get each other. And I genuinely like that dude, so much so that if I needed a favor, I'd call him. And I think he'd call me, too. Turns out, much like me, Jason is just a quiet guy. He was dragged through the mud a couple of times and I felt bad for him, because he's a quality person under the persona. First impressions aren't always right. Not about Jason, not about me, not really about anyone.

Jason aside, some artists lack any sense of humor about themselves whatsoever. I can live with that. It's very important to me to keep some sense of equilibrium between my guests and me while we are on air. I'm not bigger than they are, and they're not bigger than I am. Nor are they bigger than the listeners and fans. We are all people. Except for Garth Brooks, who's the greatest of all time. He's bigger than us all. Yeah, Garth Brooks stands alone.

I've interviewed Garth Brooks (I can't call the guy who's sold 134 million albums "Garth," but Mr. Brooks seems a little formal, so I'm just going to keep going with Garth Brooks) a few times now. I couldn't believe that the first time he came in the studio he brought a guitar and played whatever songs we wanted. By pretty much any metric you can come up with, from album sales to monster arena tours, the man is bigger than any musician living or dead, including Madonna, Michael Jackson, Sinatra, and even the King himself, Elvis. He was just the nicest guy, though, which is what 95 percent of country music stars are. Then, at the end of his visit, he *gave* me his guitar, which he signed. Oh my god. It was such an amazing experience that although I often listen back to segments of my show in order to figure what I could have done better, I didn't listen to this interview. I wanted to preserve the memory of how great it was in my mind. I didn't want to ruin it by focusing on a question I should have asked or a word I stumped on. (I've only ever done that on two other interviews: *Clerks* director Kevin Smith and my first interview years ago, with John Mayer. But Garth Brooks is definitely the most sacred.)

In my apartment I have a wall of guitars that are hung the way I guess other people hang art. That's where I keep the guitar Garth Brooks gave me. There are also guitars from John Mayer, Ben Harper, and Darius Rucker from Hootie and the Blowfish, who came in as a guest my first week in Nashville. (I no longer take guitars from guests, but I buy one or two a week for artists to sign and then I give them to charity.) There's one over in the corner on the wall from Dierks Bentley, whose song "I Hold On" we really championed on our show. After it went to No. 1, he wrote all the lyrics on a guitar and gave it to me. Eric Paslay, who was a big songwriter in Nashville before he went solo, did the same thing with his first single, "Friday Night." I was the first to play the single, which also hit No. 1. So I have a guitar with every lyric to that song written on it. It's quite special to me. In the land of constant competition that is show business, things like that are still pretty awesome.

Dierks and Eric are just a couple of the artists *The Bobby Bones Show* has helped hit the charts. When I say this, I'm not bragging about myself (well, maybe just a little: I do have a keen ear for awesomeness) but rather about our listeners, because they're the ones who buy the music and make the hits. It took about a year for our radio show to influence the charts, but since then it's crazy how loyal and how trustworthy the listeners of my radio show have become.

One of the most gratifying chart-toppers who have come through our doors is Chris Janson. Although he'd written songs for the likes of Tim McGraw, Chris got dropped from his own recording contract. He was playing bars and struggling, like so many musicians in Nashville. Talent is everywhere, all the time in this city. Everybody is a musician, singer, and/or songwriter. And I'm not talking about second-rate guitar players or people who need Auto-Tune to sound good. If you aren't the best of the best, you will be chewed up and spit out here. You can go to any bar on any street and watch somebody who's amazing and only working for tips. So Nashville is crowded with people struggling to make it in country music—and yet talented people from all over the country still move here year after year.

With Chris, I kept inviting him into the studio, even though I got some heat for it. A show of our scope is only supposed to have guests with as much mass appeal as possible, and that means at minimum a record deal. But anytime we did some sort of feature with artists, we would always invite Chris in, because he was our first-ever guest and just a guy. Most important, though, he is a great musician. That's an important element to our listeners' loyalty; we don't push bad music on our show for any agenda, so they know they can trust us.

Anyway, one night Chris e-mailed me a song with the message "Hey, tell me what you think. I just put it up on iTunes myself." I liked it and wanted to play it the next morning, so I e-mailed it to my producer, Ray, asking him to put it up on my screen in case I had time to play it.

We ended up with about forty-five seconds to kill before a

commercial break that morning in early 2015, so I said to our listeners, "I got an e-mail from our buddy Chris Janson . . ." Then I played just a snippet of the song "Buy Me a Boat."

I thought the song was good, but my tastes don't always mix perfectly with everyone else's. Well, this time they did, because "Buy Me a Boat" exploded. Within thirty minutes of me playing forty-five seconds of the song, it went from nonexistent to one of the top downloads on iTunes. So then I played the full song (again risking pissing off the higher-ups at iHeartRadio, because you're taught not to play untested music on a national level), and by the end of the day, it was the No. 1 song in iTunes country and in the Top 10 on the pop chart, too!

Of course, every record label was after Chris immediately then. Chris wound up signing with Warner Bros., which put out his debut album, named after "Buy Me a Boat," its lead single, which went to No. 1 on the Billboard country charts. The album debuted at No. 4 on the Top Country Albums chart and No. 18 on the Billboard 200. The song, which sold more than 805,000 units, went gold, and Chris landed an opening spot on Toby Keith's summer tour. The day his song climbed to No. 1, Chris sent me a note: "None of this would have happened if it wasn't for you opening that e-mail, listening to my song, and playing it on the air. You got me a deal."

If "Buy Me a Boat" didn't convince me of the power of our listeners and the show, then "Girl Crush" really nailed it for me. Little Big Town—the band featuring Karen Fairchild, Kimberly Schlapman, Jimi Westbrook, and Phillip Sweet, all on vocals— had released their sixth studio album, *Pain Killer*. The single they were pushing was a party song called "Day Drinking." But as soon as I heard "Girl Crush," which was a deep track, I knew *that* was the real single.

It's slow, and right now ballads are out of favor in country music, but I thought the song, with Karen on lead vocals, was different, in a good way, from anything else out there. So the next morning, I took to the airwaves to introduce the song to my listeners. I don't want to sound like a broken record or a jerk, but "Girl Crush" instantly skyrocketed up the iTunes charts to the Top 5 that morning. Because of that segment, they put it out as the album's second single after "Day Drinking." And the rest is history. "Girl Crush," with sales of nearly 1.5 million in the U.S., literally made *Billboard* history when it spent eleven weeks at No. 1.

I should have gotten a shout-out by country music programmers everywhere, right? Nope. I created blowback. Apparently the song's topic, one woman's obsession with another, was too risqué for country radio. Playing lyrics like "I want to taste her lips / Yeah, 'cause they taste like you" were "promoting the gay agenda," according to some angry listeners and station managers. Frightened program directors refused to play the song. Although so many country music fans downloaded the song that it was No. 4 on iTunes, it was only No. 33 in radio airplay rankings because DJs were afraid to play a song about lesbians. (Meanwhile the band says unequivocally that the song isn't about lesbians. Who cares? I like lesbians.)

When I had Little Big Town in the studio, I went on a rant. "Is it frustrating to you that here is your song—that is one of the top ten sellers for weeks and weeks and weeks—and people on the radio are still afraid to play it because they think it's a 'lesbian song'?" I asked. "It would drive me insane!"

My bosses weren't happy about me screaming on air at the country radio industry, which paid me my salary, for being small-minded hypocrites. But I wasn't worried. I knew the listeners had my back.

They always do, which is why I can say what I believe—or maybe it's the other way around. Because I say what I think, the listeners always have my back. Either way, I have enough strong support to take up the issues important to me.

When it comes to the current country music industry, the biggest issue for me is the prevalence of what's known as "bro country." If you aren't up on country music, that's the kind of song where a male singer belts out lyrics along the lines of "Hey, girl, get up and dance on my truck; I want to watch you while I drink whiskey." And I hate it, and I have since I started working in this format. By the time this book comes out, it could have gone the way of the boy band, but right now I am still praying for its death.

In addition to being an epicenter of talent, Nashville is also a factory. With people who just write songs and others who just sing them, the whole thing can get pretty formulaic. There's a particular songwriter voice, where everything sounds about the same, which is male dominated and really demeaning toward women. Plus, the radio industry is infiltrated with dudes while women are often pushed to the side.

I speak to women daily. Not only was I raised surrounded by women—my mom, grandma, and sisters—but they are also a huge part of my audience. I might as well be a woman. So at a time when there are so few female artists getting to the top of the charts (unless you're Miranda Lambert or Carrie Underwood), I've been focusing on really strong females inside of country music.

For the last two years I've done a whole week devoted to great women in country music on the show. Each day of that week, we choose one or two different females to highlight and bring into the studio. We try to pick those who are less well known (which isn't hard in today's country climate). Instead of bringing in the superstars with tons of hits, we have invited great contemporary country artists like Lindsay Ell, Maddie and Tae, Jana Kramer, Cam, Ashley Monroe, and many others who aren't getting their fair shake because they don't have a ding-dong and sing about tapping kegs.

In this arena, I might be proudest of Kelsea Ballerini, whose debut single, "Love Me Like You Mean It," reached No. 1 on the Billboard Country Airplay chart in July 2015. That made her the first solo female country musician to have her first single hit No. 1 since Carrie Underwood. The craziest part is that the Raging Idiots were a tiny bit helpful in launching her career. The first-ever tour that she went on was with my band (I should confess that I use that term loosely; we're really more like a bunch of buddies who get onstage and play). We took Kelsea out with us for a few months, and I had her on the radio show a ton, too. She was going to get there anyway; we just sped up the process a bit.

I've only ever really been in a couple of feuds, but I regret them because in each I was the bigger jackass. One all started when *Nashville Lifestyles* put out an issue devoted to "Nashville's 10 Most Beautiful People," and—now don't laugh—I was named one of those people! Nobody was more stunned by my inclusion than I was. But for a solid month while the magazine was on newsstands, every artist who came on the show made fun of me relentlessly.

I didn't mind the ribbing. I know I'm no Brad Pitt or Ryan

Gosling, so I'd rather have someone make fun of me than congratulate me. Still, when *Country Weekly* released its list of "Country's Sexiest Men of 2014," I said on air, "I don't care who they are. I'm making fun of every one of them, because I've been getting it like crazy." Fair is fair.

I went at it really hard on everyone in that list. But hard in the least malicious way possible. "Toby Keith! Who created this list? The Keith family?" I joked on air. To which the country superstar sent me a signed picture of himself that read, "You wish you were this pretty." I laughed about that for a month.

It wasn't meant to be malicious. I like Toby a lot. In fact, the Raging Idiots opened up for him during a tour date of his in Washington, D.C. We had been in Boston for a station event when he called to ask if we would do the gig. We were really surprised he wanted the Raging Idiots, and I had no idea what happened to his original opening act. But I didn't ask any questions. With twenty thousand people at the venue, it was the biggest stage we'd ever been on. Toby even sent his plane to pick us up in Boston! After the Raging Idiots played, he called me out onstage and I played "Red Solo Cup" with him. (I held a Red Solo cup empty onstage while everyone else in the audience held theirs filled with beer.)

I thought everyone would have a sense of humor like Toby Keith. Gary Allan thought it was funny when I skewered him as a sexy man of country. I even made fun of Luke Bryan. And I love Luke.

When I busted on Keith Urban, he also got the humor in it. But then again Keith is one of the really great humans on the planet. As famous as he is, though, he's just a normal dude. (His wife, Nicole Kidman, who's just as nice, told me, "We listen to the show every morning.") When he found out that I had never seen *Dog Day Afternoon,* the classic film starting Al Pacino, he sent it to me on iTunes. Even though he's always saying, "Let me come sit in with the Raging Idiots," I *never* let him, because I don't ever want people to feel like they have to do anything for me. (Although I did sing a duet with Carrie Underwood during a Raging Idiots concert at the Ryman in Nashville. Volunteering to be a secret guest, she played with the house band, which someone of her magnitude just doesn't do. But Carrie is so laid-back and cool. I don't get intimidated performing with big stars, but when Carrie started singing, it was like a whole different thing. She was so good it was like an alien was singing or something.)

Although I wouldn't let Keith stoop down to Raging Idiots level, I did let him paint a picture for St. Jude's, something that I did myself to raise money for the children's hospital. Since then, a bunch of musicians have done the same, but Keith was the first artist to make one. If I need something, he's always there. And he doesn't have to do anything. 'Cause he's Keith Urban. And he let me make fun of his looks.

But back to my stupid feud. The one Sexiest Man of Country who didn't find my particular brand of humor amusing was Chris Young (and I thought I went the lightest on him, because I really didn't know him that well).

"Here's the thing about Chris Young," I said, "He was an extremely good-looking dude about fifteen pounds ago. Like model good looking. If he'd drop fifteen . . ." I was probably even kinder, but you get it.

A lot of people reacted a lot worse than I had ever expected.

I wish I wouldn't have said it in hindsight. I didn't think what I said was that bad, but if it upset him that much, I wanted to apologize.

I got my chance when I saw Chris at the end of a Brad Paisley concert. We were both backstage when I said to him, "Listen. I'm really sorry about what I said. That was me making a bad joke. And if it hurt your feelings, I'm really sorry. You should come back on the show. I hate that it happened." His response was to roll his eyes.

Maybe I hadn't picked the right place and time. There were a lot of people milling around backstage in that moment. Maybe, I thought, he didn't hear me. If I wasn't sure about his dislike for me at Brad's concert, he didn't leave any doubt when I next saw him, at the Academy of Country Music Awards.

Rachel and I were already dating by this point, so we went together to the annual award ceremony, where I sat with her and the rest of her band, Gloriana. When Chris came up to where we were sitting, I tried to apologize for the second time. "Hey, man," I said. "I'm really sorry about what happened. I know we didn't really get to talk about it. I hate that it happened. If you ever want to come back on the show . . . I'm really sorry . . . I was a total jackass."

He looked at me straight in the eyes, then looked away, and without saying anything, walked off. At least so it seemed to me. Maybe he didn't hear me again. It was in a loud room. And I still felt like a big ol' idiot.

I didn't know the first thing about Chris Young, but he didn't know me either. He had no clue how hard it was for me to say sorry once, let alone twice. And I also had no idea how bad that joke went over with him. Yeah, you can't joke on the air five hours a day, five days a week, and hit a home run every time. I had struck out. And hard.

Here's how I reacted to this whole thing; we stopped saying his name on the air for five months. Like a petty despot, I had an outright ban on those two words, "Chris Young." I realize now it was really sophomoric of me, but if you've been reading this book, I suppose that's not so surprising. I have done some really dumb stuff that I regret.

Chris, if you're reading this. I apologize. You don't have to accept it. But at least we aren't in a loud room. I am a big idiot. And will continue to be.

I don't react this way only to famous people either. Anyone can make me feel less than angry. I've been known to read mean Facebook posts from listeners out loud on air. It doesn't matter if it is a journalist writing an article that says something negative about me or some random Internet post, I'm always taken right back to those childhood days of being bullied.

Here I was with the biggest radio show in country music, working with my best friends every day, getting to ask famous musicians whatever questions I wanted, dating a pretty country music star, making more money than I ever dreamed of, and yet I still carried that old chip on my shoulder. I was so worried of going back to my old way of life—basically not having anything or anyone—that I overreacted when I felt threatened in any way. In a funny kind of knee-jerk reaction, I stood up for myself *too* much.

I know people liked me, as an entertainer, because of the raw quality of emotion I brought to the air in what is typically such a phony medium. It was good radio, but was it good for me?

10

A TOTAL NIGHTMARE

I am never late. Ever. To anything. If I am late, that's because something is wrong—like I've-been-hit-by-a-car wrong. But that's never happened, so as I said, I'm never late.

I wish I could say the same thing about the rest of the people on my show.

Although I come in anytime between 3 and 4 A.M., depending on what's happening that day, the official start time for everyone else is 4:30 A.M. so that we have a half hour to organize ourselves before the show starts at 5 A.M. Central.

Lateness is one of my biggest pet peeves. I get so mad when someone is not on time. I'm even madder at myself if for some reason I can't be somewhere when I said I would. It's the most disrespectful thing I can think of; if people are late, it's as if they're saying their time is more important than whomever they've kept waiting. So when people on the show started to con-sistently come in late, I called a meeting with my staff and gave it to them straight.

"Okay, this being late stuff is out of control," I said. "It's totally inconsiderate to the rest of the team. Over and over and over again?"

If that wasn't clear enough, I made a new rule.

"If you're one second late, you're going home."

After I gave the "be here or be sent home" speech, some of them still couldn't be on time for more than a couple of days. Three days after our meeting, two people who shall remain nameless showed up late. By only a few minutes, but it was still late. And this was after we HAD JUST TALKED ABOUT LATENESS NOT BEING TOLERATED. I was so pissed.

"I told you, you have to be there at four thirty, not four thirty-one," I said. "I can't make a rule and not enforce it. So, go home."

They couldn't believe it when it happened, but I sent two peo-ple home from the show.

I know that was a hard-ass thing to do, but I don't know any other way to be. It's how I am with myself. I've got to be effective with time management if I'm going to manage all the projects I juggle—from radio to my band to writing this book! (At the time I was only speaking to a couple of people who couldn't make it into work on time. But actually, as I write this, everyone except Ray has had an incident of being late within the last thirty days. And it still makes me mad.)

Getting everything done for *The Bobby Bones Show* takes laser focus and a constant vigilance when it comes to time. Cutting commercials for sponsors in all the cities we are in; doing liners for each of our ninety affiliate stations where I read the name of each station and anything else sent in to localize the show; and recording the weekend countdown is all in a day's work for me. So everything with me is about what can I shoehorn into my time in the studio so that I'm not there for ten hours a day, while still completing it all at a high level?

I've found a pattern where in the early hours before the show, I start rattling off station liners for all the affiliates. When I'm done with that, I'll do some local segments for certain cities. Then it's usually time to hop on the air and start the show. At the first break, I start recording the countdown for *Country Top 30*, my four-hour weekend country music program. Then we're back on live. Do the show. Break. Do some commercials. Break. More countdown. Back on.

It just doesn't stop. From 5 A.M. to 10 A.M., I literally don't stop. I can't even go to the bathroom. There isn't a single forty-five-second window for me to get up and pee. And that's how I like it. For as many hours a day and years of my life as I've been doing this, it is still a rush. This is my comfort zone. When I'm sitting behind a console board, controlling all those buttons, I feel my best. That's why even though most people in my world don't run their own board, push their own buttons, I still do. Most personalities just have their microphone and producers who run everything for them. Not me. I want to be able to control every slide, every commercial, every single song that comes through. I'm not bragging or showing off; it's actually the opposite. I should be able to let it go, at least a little bit. And I try. But I feel like it won't get done right unless I do it myself.

I'm a control freak. I like knowing that if something gets screwed up, I have only myself to blame. And on October 24, 2014, I screwed up big time.

Now, I have to be very careful about what I write here. Even in a joking manner. I got in a lot of trouble with the U.S. government (you know, *those* guys) because of something I did on the air that day. Something that was a total accident. Something that ended with me getting my company hit with a fine of one million dollars. Let's just call it the Million-Dollar Bad Thing. I am so nervous even to write about it that I'm just going to say, google "Bobby Bones Fined $1 Million." What a terrible writer I am! I ask you to pay good money for a book in which I require that you google something to get the full story. Listen, I'm not getting in trouble with Uncle Sam again for a paragraph of a book that maybe no one is even going to read anyway.

I'm joking now, but at the time that the Million-Dollar Bad Thing happened, I wasn't laughing. In fact I was panicked that I was about to be fired. Not even when Charlamagne Tha God, DJ for one of the other biggest morning shows in the country, out of New York City, and a mentor and friend, sent me hundreds of emojis laughing so hard they were crying could I calm down. And if Charlamagne couldn't get me out of my head, no one could.

I first met Charlamagne at an iHeartRadio Music Festival several years earlier when the company we both worked for took its top people for an off-site where we were stuck together for three days. That's when I became friends with Charlamagne and Lisa Kennedy Montgomery (aka Kennedy, the original conservative MTV VJ now turned Fox Business Network host). I don't use the word "friend" lightly, and I'm even stingier with the term in media circles, but Charlamagne, Kennedy, and I became a tight little triangle of friends.

I particularly identified with Charlamagne, who grew up poor in South Carolina and, like me, had to grind out a career path for himself. Ever since that festival where we met, we talk all the time on the phone, sometimes three times a week. We motivate each other in our work, because we are both examples that where you're from doesn't have to determine who you become.

So it was no surprise, then, that after the Million-Dollar Bad Thing happened, he was one of the first and only people to reach out to me.

"It sucks right now, but fight through it," he said, "because this is what legends are made of."

I appreciated Charlamagne—I always do. But even he couldn't get through to me with this one. I felt like a complete loser. People trusted me to do the biggest show this format's ever seen—and I let this happen? It wasn't like I went on a creative limb and fell off. What happened was just a dumb technical error that shook my foundation. And usually nothing, *nothing* messes with me.

Whenever I do something on a massive level—like when I hosted morning TV with Kelly Ripa or some of the biggest music managers in country came to see one of my Raging Idiots shows—I don't experience it as pressure and get nervous. Instead it's time to compete and win—and I get pumped. Now, sometimes I don't win. But I always try to.

The Million-Dollar Bad Thing rocked me pretty hard, though, not only because of the enormous sum of money iHeartMedia was facing in terms of FCC fines but because I let down the same people who had taken such a big chance on me. Unlike many of the other disappointments I have experienced, this was one I couldn't compartmentalize and put away.

Work wasn't the only thing in my life that was out of control at that moment. After Rachel and I dated for about a year, her team convinced her that she needed to stop seeing me because it was ruining her career. I had predicted this moment months before. "You know what's going to happen?" I had told her. "They're going to tell you that I'm hurting your career. And maybe I am. If you date the biggest radio personality on iHeartRadio, you may be penalized by Cumulus or CBS."

Rachel didn't want to hear it. She told me how much she loved me and wanted to stay together. But I cut it off. I couldn't stand the idea that there was even a chance I was hurting someone's career for a relationship that probably wasn't going to last anyway—no matter how good it was. It didn't matter that we laughed all the time. Or that we started as friends and morphed into a relationship in the best possible way. I knew no one would stay with me long term.

As soon as Rachel and I split up, I found myself in a bizarre scenario. For the first time in the short history of Bobby Estell, women, and lots of them, were interested in me. It was crazy. Women, real-life women, wanted to go out with *me*. So, like a man who's been starving for years and is taken to an all-you-can-eat buffet, I dated everyone. At the height of this small blip in an otherwise flatlined social life, I went out with six or seven girls—all at once.

They were actresses and musicians, famous folks, but I never talked about any of it on the air. I would have, but it was their business. That's always my rule with what I'll say on air—I'm not going to talk about *you*; I'm going to talk about *me*. And then, if you're okay with me talking about you, I'll talk about you, too. But in terms of the women I was seeing during this period, I didn't need everyone to know I was dating them. I especially didn't want the women I was dating to know about each other!

Keeping my stories straight was the hardest part of being a Casanova. (The second-hardest part was typing that line.) I had to remember what I had or hadn't told to each woman. Sometimes I'd repeat myself. Other times I made a reference to something she'd never heard before. It was a mess. Again, I didn't have tons of experience with women, and certainly never juggled multiple relationships, so this was all Louis-and-Clark stuff to me. One area where I nailed it, however, was my phone system.

I've only had one phone number for the past fifteen years, and I don't keep two phones. So I came up with the idea to put the women I was seeing into my phone under the names of old Cubs baseball players. In my twisted code, a woman whose name started with M appeared as Mark Grace—the Cubs' first baseman—when she texted. I could be out for a romantic dinner with said Mark Grace and suddenly my phone is blowing up with Andre Dawson, who played right field; Shawon Dunston (short-stop); Ryne Sandberg (second baseman); I had the whole 1989 National League East's winning team sending me text messages.

It was fun for a minute, but more as a diversion than anything else. It wasn't like I sowed my wild oats. I went on lots of dates, held lots of hands, paid for lots of dinners, and that's about it. In truth, I didn't go out with any of my Cubs more than a handful of times. We'd make out a little bit and then become friends. My fear of getting an STD or a woman pregnant slammed the brakes on getting freaky. Sad but true.

In the end, my serial dating was more wearing and exhausting than anything else. I couldn't even find fun in dating beautiful and occasionally really famous women. Everything seemed to be draining—even work—mostly because I had stopped sleeping. The Million-Dollar Bad Thing was out there and hanging over my head. At this point, the dollar amount still hadn't been decided, but I was told it was going to be a Five-Million-Dollar Bad Thing. I beat myself up about it over and over while I lay in bed at night.

The stress pushed me over some kind of edge and I found myself reliving a series of traumatic events that had happened since moving to Nashville and which until this point I had kept bottled up.

The first messed-up thing happened after I'd been in Nashville for only three days. On my company's suggestion, I had moved into a fancy, gated neighborhood right on a golf course. I thought it was way too expensive a place to live, but they insisted. "It doesn't matter. You've had too much crap happen to you," one exec said, referring not only to the crazed lunatic with a knife who had been waiting for me outside the radio station in Austin but also to repeated death threats against me.

I wasn't even that controversial. I talked about not getting girls and my dog, Dusty. Still, people wanted to mess with me. (After a person repeatedly called to say, "If you walk outside of the radio station, I'm going to kill you," the station had to build a whole bulletproof-glass room in the front of the building and hire security.) So I moved into my super safe house in Nashville with twenty-four-hour security. And three days later (I hadn't even started to unpack my boxes) I was asleep when everything went insane—my phone, my computer, and my sense of well-being.

As it turned out, about ten houses down a guy apparently had murdered his wife and was now on foot in my gated super safe neighborhood. SWAT teams had invaded and were shouting through bullhorns for everyone to lock up and stay inside, because the man was armed and dangerous. They caught him in the woods a day later, but it proved to me that anything can happen anywhere. (And I soon moved.)

The wife murderer was an unfortunate but random event. Others were directed *at me*. Next up were two agent-type guys who showed up at my front door and showed their badges.

"Do you mind if we come in?" one of them asked.

Did I have a choice? Not really; they were IRS agents.

"You've been compromised," one agent said. "Someone who works for us has hacked into your files."

They showed me a picture and I recognized the woman instantly. A huge fan of the show, she had come to a number of our live events. Because her work computer was monitored, they were aware when she breached security by looking into my files. Of course they were! What kind of employee of the IRS doesn't know they are going to be caught if they dig into people's personal information? A dumb one, that's who. The agents asked me if I wanted to press charges. "Yes," I said, and never heard anything more about the woman again.

That might have been my last interaction with that woman, but it wasn't my last with government agents. Shortly after the IRS showed up at my house, two *other* secret agent types showed up at my studio while I was in the middle of my radio show. This time, though, it was immediately clear the situation was a lot more serious.

"Get off the air right now," one of them said.

"Well, two guys with suits walked in," I said on air. "I guess I've got to go."

I hit a song and told someone, "Just play songs till I'm done."

The two men escorted me to a room in the station and said, "We want to know about the threats you've posted to the President of the United States." Or something like that. I was so freaked out my ears were ringing, which made it hard to hear.

"I did not threaten the President of the United States," I insisted to them. But in my head I tried to remember what stupid thing I had said on air that could have been misconstrued as a threat. It was hard to think, though, when I was pretty sure I was about to get a one-way ticket to Guantánamo.

If I was freaked out before, when they put up paper to block out the window in the door and started to press me pretty hard, I was downright panicked. Even though the men in suits identified themselves, I honestly don't remember what agency they were a part of—FBI, I guess? They could have been Secret Service. I was so scared I have no idea. I learned that the government doesn't mess around. I cracked a couple of jokes, but they weren't funny to anybody but me. And then I stopped cracking jokes. The government; they don't play.

"You didn't write this message to the president saying, 'I'm going to kill you, N-word'?"

Once I realized it wasn't something I said on air but a written message, I breathed a sigh of relief. I sometimes say things I don't remember because I have to talk so much. "Guys, I absolutely did not do this," I said.

The person who *did* send that threatening message to the White House was a listener, who had created an e-mail account under my name. As it turned out, the agents knew I wasn't the person behind it and were just doing their due diligence. (If that was just doing their due diligence, I'd hate to experience a real interrogation.)

Being a public person comes with an inherent share of craziness, but I found that each threatening event I experienced built on the next to create a sense of constant anxiety. From being robbed outside a club in Little Rock to being jumped outside of work in Austin by the man with a knife to my IRS files getting hacked to multiple death threats, I struggled to maintain my equilibrium. I didn't want to sink into paranoia and constant worry that the world is dangerous and ultimately against me. But every time something bad happened, no matter how much I had worked on myself in therapy and how far I'd come in life, it was like I went right back to the place from which I started.

Whenever I slid back into this bad state of mind the nightmares returned. These were the same ones that I had for weeks after the incident in Austin in the early morning hours outside the studio. I would dream that I was lying in bed—the same bedroom, the same bed that I was actually lying in. In the nightmare someone with a gun was breaking into my room. It was always the exact same thing, down to the same gun. The worst part, however, was that because the dream happened in my bedroom, when I woke up in that same room, I felt like I was still in the middle of my nightmare. Only it was real life.

That happens about forty, fifty days in a row and you are going to be exhausted.

After the Million-Dollar Bad Thing happened, all the other events rushed back—and so did the nightmares. I stopped sleeping altogether.

I have never been a great sleeper, because I'm always worried that I'm going to oversleep and miss work. And if I miss work, I'm going to lose my job. Back to square one. I sleep with my laptop in my bed. My phone is my alarm. And I sleep with another alarm set to back up my phone. Still, to make sure I don't oversleep, I check the clock three or four times a night. I'm not sure I remember what a good night's rest feels like.

Still, this was a whole other kind of unrest. Every night I had the same nightmare, over and over again. Waking up with my heart racing, there was no way I could get back to sleep. So I'd just stay up and work. I got to the point where I couldn't sleep for more than an hour at a time. Then it seemed as if I didn't sleep at all.

It was murder, getting out of bed at 3 A.M. and feeling like crap every day. Because I don't like to put any kind of drug in my body, and don't do coffee, it was sheer gut and will that got me through this show. And I got sick and stayed sick, because of the lack of sleep.

I was never late (have I mentioned that I don't do that?), but that didn't mean I was doing a great job. In that period when I didn't know how much I was going to get fined by the FCC and I wasn't sleeping, *The Bobby Bones Show* went through a really sour time. Months went by when the ratings were terrible. It wasn't even that our listeners were angry with me for the Million-Dollar Bad Thing. The trouble made the news, but mainly it was just in media circles. It was such a blip, hardly anyone in the mainstream knew about it. No, the bad ratings were simply due to the fact that I wasn't doing a good show.

This was the lowest point I had ever reached in my life—and that's when you go and ask for help.

My therapist had suggested a few times over the course of our working together that I consider taking antidepressants. It wasn't that I was depressed; I was just never happy. I never got out of being sad—if that makes sense. Still, I was terrified of taking pills. I don't like taking pills. And for good reason.

The obsessive nature I inherited from my mom was always lurking in the background. Like I said, if it wasn't golf or poker, then it was Subway sandwiches or working out. I had to work out at the exact same time, for the exact same amount of time, every day of the week, or I didn't want to work out at all. I started eating right, which meant no cheat dates, ever. For four months, I didn't touch bread or sweets, and I love eating bread and sweets. But I couldn't do it. I can't do anything in moderation.

I wish I were able to use alcohol to be more comfortable in social situations, because I'm very uncomfortable socially. I'm always quiet, shy, reserved. Even now. It's odd, because I talk for hours each day to millions of people and perform live in front of thousands. If I'm onstage at a Raging Idiots concert or doing a television show, I'm not unnerved because it's a performance. But real-life interactions, I'm not good at. So when I'm not performing, I mainly keep to myself, sometimes not even leaving my bedroom.

Did that mean I was depressed? I wasn't sure, but I didn't want to end up like my mom, so at a certain point I decided to talk to my doctor about taking antidepressants. I was so nervous, however, that I needed more than just the opinion of my therapist, even though I trusted her implicitly. I had three months of conversations with my medical doctor, too, who didn't push me either way as I asked tons and tons of questions.

"Am I going to be out-of-control up?"

"Will I be the same person?"

"Am I going to put on weight?"

"Am I going to be able to think the same?"

"Will I get addicted?"

He laid out the benefits and risks until I was ready to make a decision. I wound up taking them for three or four months, during which time I didn't notice any perceptible change at all. I know it takes a while for that stuff to kick in, and that you have to work closely with a doctor who really understands the right dosage and medication for you. But my ambivalence meant that I wasn't all that committed to the process. So I just stopped again, with the doctor's help.

Here I was, my life seemingly crumbling around me because I was unable to sleep. I knew that my inability to sleep came from deeper, darker demons that I needed to wrestle with, but in order to do that I needed to get some sleep!

I went back to my doctor and he prescribed sleeping pills, more precisely a pill called Edluar. Again, we talked all about it, the pros and cons, my fear of abuse. But I was at the end of my rope, and the fear of not being able to work outweighed my anxiety over becoming addicted to sleeping pills. So I started to take them, one or two every day.

It wasn't miraculous, but I did sleep—without nightmares. Many sleeping pills don't get you to REM sleep, the most restful type during which you dream, and this was one of those kinds of pills. So when I woke up, it didn't feel like I had had a full rest. But it was better than dreaming I was getting murdered in my own bed or not falling asleep at all. I was able to function, but if I didn't take a pill, the nightmares returned. I wanted to stay fixed. So I kept taking them and taking them and taking them.

Then on May 19, 2015, the FCC finally made its determination about the Million-Dollar Bad Thing that had happened seven months earlier. iHeartMedia, which agreed to a three-year compliance and reporting plan, was fined the million dollars.

One million dollars is nothing to sneeze at, but the relief of having a resolution was priceless. I was deeply fortunate and grateful that my company paid the fine willingly and didn't ask for my head on a platter by way of compensation. As if a mega Band-Aid had been ripped from a wound, I was ready to heal. I said to myself, "You know what? Things really sucked for a while, and I'm not going to let them suck anymore."

It was time to change my attitude and get back to it.

By this point, we had fallen all the way from number one to out of the top ten in ratings. We bottomed out because *I* had bottomed out. If I didn't fix the situation, *The Bobby Bones Show* was going to be over. Just as I had caused the problem, I had to fix it.

I talked to my CEO, Bob Pittman, the man who gave me my current contract and had invested so much in me over the past couple of years.

"Listen," I said. "I'm going to turn this around. I'm not even going to say, 'Trust me'; I'm just going to do it."

And we did. We turned it around. It was one step at a time, one hour at a time, one show at a time. I started to crank up the machine again, keeping notes every day, all day, of things that popped into my head:

♪ My grandma getting arrested once for playing bingo in a van

♪ New smart chips in credit cards

♪ How Amy can't keep a secret

♪ The prevalence of farts in cartoons on Nickelodeon

Anything that seemed interesting or I had an opinion on, I wrote down in the Notepad app on my phone. There are thousands of them there now.

Slowly but surely, I started to right the ship through good old-fashioned hard work—but work done with joy and lightness—until we were back to number one in Nashville.

Being on top again was great, but the real success was what I learned from the whole experience. I had started to get, as my grandma would say, "too big for my britches." I was making money, sticking it in the face of my old bullies and the detractors with high ratings and awards, dating lots of girls. And then I made a technical error that put my career in jeopardy, sapped my confidence, and led me to stop sleeping altogether. I thought of myself as a great innovator and then right quick, I almost lost my job.

I saw which relationships—not just romantic ones—remain when times are bad. You know, who sticks around when things are rough. There were a lot of folks who just went peace-out on us when we were down. I won't forget that. The most profound and inspiring lesson I came away with, however, was that as rotten as life and your situation may seem, if you just put your head down and continue to fight through, you'll come out the other side.

I do believe that the Million-Dollar Bad Thing, as hard as it knocked me down, saved me. It taught me not only to stay humble and continue to work hard, but also to appreciate what I've got.

Once I dug my show out of the ratings hole I had created, I turned toward digging myself out of the chemical dependency I found myself in. I had to get off the sleeping pills, which I had continued to take each and every night. I announced to my doctor, "I am not taking these anymore," and like I had done with golf, poker, Subway sandwiches, etc., I went cold turkey with the sleeping pills.

The difference with the pills was, when I stopped playing cards or golf, I didn't go through any withdrawal. With the pills, however, I got really sick.

As soon as I stopped taking my sleeping medication, my body went crazy. It had become used to getting something every night that suddenly was no longer there. I vomited violently for days, shaking and convulsing so badly I couldn't walk or see straight. It made me feel really terrible for people who try to get off drugs like heroin or OxyContin. I was just detoxing from sleeping pills and I felt like I was going to die. It gave me some empathy for why people fail to get clean. Sadly, it made me understand my mom a little more.

Just like with everything else, I fought through the withdrawal and emerged on the other side, and once I was back on my feet, I vowed I would never go back to the place I had just been.

11

EVERY DAY IS A GOOD DAY

I was driving down the small country road leading into Mountain Pine on an overcast afternoon in late May 2015 when I noticed in the distance a green road sign with white writing on it. I hadn't seen a sign on that road for a while; I think it had been stolen or something. I had no idea what the name of the road was, either—probably Truck Road 379 or whatever. It didn't really matter, since there's only one way into and out of Mountain Pine.

As I got close enough to make out the writing, I couldn't believe what I saw. The sign read:

MOUNTAIN PINE, POP. 772
WELCOME TO THE BOYHOOD HOME OF BOBBY BONES

The new addition to the sign came as a total shock. I was back home to speak at the high school graduation ceremony and to present the scholarship I had created to its first recipient. But I had no idea that Mountain Pine had done this.

I immediately pulled over to check it out. There it was for whoever happened to find themselves going to this tiny town in Arkansas: "The Boyhood Home of Bobby Bones." It was awesome, but also weird. I mean, I'm not dead yet. You never know what's going to happen with someone who's still alive. You should definitely never, ever name a school or institution after someone living in case that person screws up big time. All those Bill Cosby elementary schools right now are like, "Oh crap." I guess they can always take down the sign outside of Mountain Pine if I go off the rails.

Joking aside, I didn't feel like I had done enough to deserve my name on that sign. The sign outside of Hot Springs says, THE BOYHOOD HOME OF BILL CLINTON. He was the president of the United States. Me? I was Quiz Bowl captain, and I play Miley Cyrus and Brad Paisley records. It's quite the difference. Still, I wasn't going to ask them to take it down, either. It felt good to see my name up there.

The town put up the sign in tandem with my scholarship fund, which is called the Don't Be Skipping Class Scholarship. That's really the name of it. Because, as I've said, success is mostly about just showing up (and being on time), and I wanted to honor those who did just that in school.

I consider the scholarship as one of my top three accomplishments, none of which have anything to do with my career other than that they're cool things I've been able to do since becoming moderately successful. I mentioned the other two already. First there was getting my teeth fixed. I never went to the dentist until I got insurance in my twenties. So there was a lot of retro pay to pick up in the form of surgery after surgery after surgery, root canal after root canal. While it was never pleasurable, getting my teeth fixed was a big deal to me. It didn't make me prettier—as my grandma would say, "You can't polish a turd"—but having straight, nonrotten teeth (and yeah, some of them are fake) feels like I'm on the come-up. The second achievement that stands out for me was buying my mom a couple of acres on the hill for her trailer. It meant something to be able to provide for her. In the end, it didn't save her. But at least I can say she had a place to call home.

My third accomplishment, the annual scholarship that goes to a Mountain Pine high school graduate attending college, lends a helping hand to a motivated kid who probably doesn't have a lot. After I went to college, the lumber mill shut down, and that is when the town really suffered. Mountain Pine was already a place where folks struggled, but it became more so then.

Mountain Pine can feel like a forgotten place (it didn't have cell phone reception until 2015), and kids growing up there can feel forgotten in it. That's certainly how I felt. So the scholarship is doing for someone else what I wish could have been done for me.

The Don't Be Skipping Class Scholarship isn't just about grades. Any senior who is going to college creates a portfolio, which includes their grade-point average, extracurricular activities, a letter of recommendation, and a five-hundred-word essay. As I read through the first year's applications, I was looking for a good kid, who wanted to do right.

I found that with Peanuckle Jones. (Okay, that's not his real name, but since we aren't using a lot of real names in this book, I thought that was a funny one.) A lot of people wrote about how hard they worked in school. Peanuckle's essay was completely different. He wrote about how he played baseball and said that although his team hadn't won a game in four years, it didn't matter to him. He was still going to continue to play and work hard to get better even if he lost every game for the rest of his life.

I identified with him immediately. He didn't win the scholarship because he had good grades or did well on his SATs (although he did). Reading his essay I thought, Man, that is me. (That was only reinforced for me when I met Peanuckle the night of the graduation. Giving him my cell number and e-mail address, I told him to reach out if he ever needed anything. Just like I said to Deion Sanders when he gave me his number, Peanuckle made it clear he would never dare bother me by calling or e-mailing.)

In a way, the scholarship is a selfish act. I can admit it. The award is money that the winner can use in any way he or she wants. Books, tuition, anything. Want to go out and eat a few hundred times? Whatever's going to make your life slightly easier as you try to navigate through college, I GOT YOU! It feels selfish, because that is what I would have wanted when I was entering my freshman year of college. It's almost as if I'm entering a time machine, finding the younger me, and saying, "Hey, Little Bobby, I'm going to help you out."

It always comes back to me. That's a major reason I like to help people: I want to help the Me's out there. With everyone on the show and great dudes like Jason Aldean (remember—the country music star who I thought hated me when I first came to Nashville? I told you, he's my buddy now), Keith Urban, and Dierks Bentley, we have raised millions for different children's hospitals all over the country. That cause in particular always brings me back to when I was in the hospital with a ruptured spleen. We couldn't afford medical care, but someone paid my bills. And now I can help places like the hospital that took care of me.

I've often thought I should give for the sake of giving and not because it makes me feel better about an issue I've experienced. Like, I should donate to a bird refuge or something. But I guess I'm way too selfish for that. I'd much rather give Christmas presents to children whose parents can't afford them, because I can imagine how psyched a kid will be opening them up, just like I was when I was little and getting cool stuff.

I don't know that I was put here for any reason. I don't think so. But I do know that I want to leave this place better than how I found it. And the way I help best is when I have a personal connection. That's why I regularly speak to groups of people who are dealing with alcoholism or addiction. Although I've never had a drink or touched an illegal drug, I don't give any kind of moralistic speech. It's not about that. What I've found is that whenever I meet people who've been affected by substance abuse—either their own or that of someone they love—there's an inherent bond. It's almost as if you come from the same place. It's just that this place is where your pain comes from. I want others to know that if they have trouble letting go of the past or continue to struggle with that demon over and over, they aren't alone.

Despite all the success I've achieved in my career, I am just like anyone else who has a hard time coming to terms with life's disappointments. Although it's been several years since my mother passed away, I can't sell the land I bought for her. I get a bill for taxes on it every year. Meanwhile there could be someone living on it. I don't know, because I refuse to return to even look at the place.

That is definitely a metaphor for the way I've learned to cope with painful realities and emotions. I just try to shut them out. When I returned to Mountain Pine to give out the scholarship, I went to see a few people that I keep in touch with, like my friend Scotty. Then I went over to see my former stepdad, Keith, at his new house, and we decided to grab some food. In the car, he said, "I know we haven't talked about your mom since she died."

Oh no.

I would have done anything to get out of that conversation—including jump out of a car traveling sixty miles per hour. It wasn't the subject that made me nervous but the intimacy of the conversation. It could have been about anything. When someone wants to have a face-to-face exchange about feelings, I get freaked out.

"I'm really sorry, how it happened," he said.

In total he probably talked about three minutes, during which Keith said he was the one who had found her in the kitchen of her trailer. Or maybe he said someone called him to say she was dead. The fact that I don't remember is more telling than the details of who discovered my mother's body.

Again, it wasn't that we were talking about my mother's death. I get this way in a lot of one-on-one conversations. My mind races, and I lose the ability to know when to respond. I get anxious that I'm going to ruin the conversation. Fixated on figuring out the right moment to talk, I'm not able to listen to what the other person is saying. This is the exact opposite of how I am on the job.

It all stems from my fundamental lack of trust in others. It's crazy that I feel that way, since I've been the recipient of so much generosity. I'm ashamed at my good fortune when I think of all the people who have looked out for me: my grandma, my stepdad, my childhood best friend Evan, Courtney, Jay Shannon, Bob Pittman and Rod Phillips from iHeartradio, and on and on. I know, a lot of people have had it a lot worse.

But I also can't beat myself up for feeling the way I feel. When my biological father disappeared from my life at five years old, I became hardwired to expect everyone to abandon me. And for that I can never forgive him.

Nothing will change that, not even seeing him face-to-face, which I did several years ago while back in Hot Springs for Christmas. It seems absurd to say now, but I had no idea he was going to be there when I accepted an invitation for Christmas dinner at my paternal grandmother's house. It wasn't my grandmother who extended the invitation (having seen her only a handful of times in my life, I had no relationship with her). My cousins, aunt, and uncle, whom I am close to, said I should come. So I did.

As soon as I walked in, a man, a little shorter than me and a lot rougher, standing in the entryway, said to me, "Hey, did you come here to kick my ass?"

"What?" I said.

I had no idea who he was and thought maybe he was making some kind of joke. Then it hit me who was talking and I felt sick to my stomach.

I had no idea when I had seen him last. It could have been that convenience store next to Evan's house. That was twenty years ago.

I should have just left. But that's not how I do things. Instead, I laughed uncomfortably and lamely said no.

Then we sat down and proceeded to have about the most awkward hour-long holiday dinner since Christmas was invented. My dad (it pains me just to type the word "dad" in reference to the man) and I didn't say one word to each other. Uncomfortable doesn't even come close to describing this meal.

After my father left, it was easier for me to pretend that he didn't exist than to deal with my rage over his leaving. That's why I don't like when he pops up on Facebook or at Christmas dinners. I recognize that I still have a lot of anger and sadness, but I'm most comfortable expressing my emotions through my work, whether it's talking on my radio show or writing a song for the Raging Idiots.

I actually did write a song about this very issue for my band, which is best known for such profound tunes as "Everybody on Facebook Hates Me" and "Ballad of Big Head Bobby." Serious songs are not usually in my wheelhouse. In fact, I named our album *The Critics Give It 5 Stars* because I knew no critic would ever give it five stars but I still wanted people to have to say that every time they mentioned the record.

For the album, I didn't plan on writing anything more serious than my romantic ballad to the greatest love of my life, Netflix. ("I take you to the park / Sit with you on a bench / To have you there with me I don't have to be rich / Only nine dollars and ninety-nine cents / Because I have you, Netflix.") But I worked with a couple of songwriters, older guys who have been at it for twenty-five years. We weren't on the same page comedy-wise, so I told them about one idea for a song, not particularly funny, about how I always wanted to go fishing with my dad—a dad, any dad. We started talking out the story, playing some chords on

the guitar, and before we left the room, we had written "Fishin'
with My Dad."

> *It was sundown on Lake Ouachita and I was ten years old*
> *Watching a daddy teach his boy how to cast a fishing pole*
> *I remember wishing that I had what he had*
> *Just one chance to go fishing with my dad . . .*
> *Mom married a good man in the summer of '93*
> *At first I wasn't too sure about what he thought of me*
> *Till he woke me up one morning*
> *I'd never been so glad that I got to go fishing with my dad*

The autobiographical song didn't fit with the goofy tone of
the rest of the album. Not a joke to be found in this one. So
I considered giving the song away, if I could find a recording
artist interested in it. But that didn't feel right because of the
nature of the material. It was Gordon Kerr, the president of our
record label, Black River Entertainment, who encouraged me
to keep the song. "If you could have anyone in the world sing
this song with you, who would it be?" he asked me. It took me
about two seconds to come up with my answer. "Garth Brooks," I
said. Then I laughed at myself. Garth is THE GREATEST OF
ALL TIME. Why would he sing a song I wrote on a record that
I was putting out? He wouldn't—that's why.

Gordon told me that it wouldn't hurt to try. So I sent "Fishin'
with My Dad" off to Garth Brooks, thinking I had about as
much chance of getting him to sing it as I had of learning to fly.
Eventually Gordon called me into his office. He told me that
Garth Brooks had heard the song and it wasn't really what he

expected. He appreciated me sending it to him and that . . . he would love to sing on the song! It took me a second to catch up. Garth Brooks was going to sing this deeply personal song of mine for real.

Channeling my emotions through my work is what has made me successful. That's the essence of the connection to my listeners. I need them as much as they need me (probably more). Radio isn't about the music, because you can get music in a hundred places. It's being able to feel like you're with your friend. Wherever I go—Madison, Wisconsin, Sacramento, or Tampa—people come up to me like we know each other. They spend two, three, four hours with me every morning, so in a way they do. It's a huge investment in me, and I'm grateful for it.

But that tendency of mine to shove all my energy into professional endeavors doesn't enhance my life. I recently spent a whole month where between station events, Raging Idiots shows, and charity dates, I was not home for a single night. And I was relieved, because I don't really know what to do with free time. If I do get a day off, I just hang out with my dog, go for a run, and watch Netflix. Other than that, I've got nothing.

My excuse for not building a social network is that I work too much. The guys on the show are all my friends, but unlike me they've actually developed lives outside the show. Even Lunchbox got married. Dang! Sometimes I get jealous that Amy, Eddie, and now Lunchbox (dang, again) have humans that they really care about. I mean, I know they care about me, but not as much as they care about those other people. It's like there's a whole other level of caring that I'm not in on, a hidden level to Mario Bros. that I haven't quite got to yet, and I can't seem to find the cheat codes to get there.

I like to be alone and need space, but I've begun to feel a slight tug toward wanting to belong someplace or to someone. Christmas is the worst for me. Last year I decided on a whim to leave the country for the first time in my life. I was in New York right before the holidays and completely untethered by family or friends. So, two days before Christmas, I decided to hop a flight to London. I have a buddy whose dad is a cabdriver over there, so he drove me around a little bit. I got carsick sitting in the wrong side of the car, looked at some old buildings, ate a bunch of scones, and hopped a flight back. It was fine.

More than somewhere to go, I want someone to go places with. I'm in my thirties now and ready to find someone who makes me get out of my comfort zone, do things that I don't think I want to do but then once I start doing them, I realize, This isn't so bad. This is actually kind of fun.

Oh hell, I'd love to find someone to spend my life with, okay! Although I have let four or five wonderful women who I was stupid not to hang on to slip right through my fingers, I'd love to get married, or not married. I want to find that person I can have kids with and leave the door open when I go number two. I don't know if it'll ever be in the cards for me, but I sure hope so.

I know it has to start with saying "I love you." The only living creature that I've ever said "I love you" to is my dog. I know. It's sick. In my defense, Dusty has been sleeping with me since he was a puppy (he's thirteen now). He's most comfortable whenever I have a body limb laying on him, so that's how I sleep—on top of him. He accepts me as I am; even though I roll around and yell and kick and do everything while I sleep, he's used to it. I am able to love my dog because I know he's not going to leave me. He's not going to declare, "You know what? I think I've had enough of you. I've moved on." Dusty doesn't have a choice. He's got to eat, and I'm the one who feeds him.

I don't like the fact that I've never said "I love you" to a sentient being with free will, but now it's become a thing where I don't want to waste it. I want to save it, like one of those Duggar girls saving her virginity for marriage. That's how big a deal the words have become to me.

My whole adult life, everyone's said, "Eventually you'll find the right person." It's eventually now. I know by now that I'm not going to just meet "the right person" and butterflies will appear in my eyeballs and my untrusting soul will turn into light. I've been around (well, sort of, at least by a hermit's standards). If it were going to happen, it would have. I'm smart enough to know it's not an "it" thing but a "me" thing.

There are a lot of things other people do easily that are murder for me—like saying "I love you" or paying my bills. Don't get me wrong; I'm not a debtor. I *overpay* my bills all the time. So if my cell phone bill is $87, I'll pay $110 in order to build up a credit. That way if I'm ever poor again—scratch that—*when* I'm poor again, I'll have a couple of months to bounce back. Recently I had to hire a business manager, because now in addition to doing the radio show and the band I also have a TV production company and clothing line. The first thing she noticed were all these credits on my various accounts, from electric to water to my cell phone. After I explained my rationale, she turned to me and said, "No. Just no." Although it made me nervous, she cashed out all of those credits. It still makes me nervous. I'll always be a poor person, even if I have money.

But I stopped overpaying my bills, and that's progress. It

might be slow, but I do think I'm moving toward my other goals, such as being more vulnerable and positive. I'm still way too skeptical of everyone and have trouble trusting, but I'm better than I used to be.

As to my goal of being more optimistic, I'm also much better at it than I've ever been before. A big part of that has to do with the fact that in everything I do I surround myself with positive people. But just as with finding love, I know that the real transformation won't happen by some external event or other person changing me. It has to start from within.

I used to discuss my general predicament with happiness a lot with my therapist. As I said, it wasn't that I was depressed; I just never got out of being sad. Even when something good happens to me—like winning an award or becoming the country's number one country morning radio show—I kill it by thinking about the next bad thing that is surely right around the corner.

My therapist suggested that when I get good news or something cool happens to me, I should take thirty seconds and let myself be happy. To set aside half a minute and make it a moment. At first it was weird and strained, like flexing a muscle you've never used before. But after a while it got easier and I found more and more little moments to enjoy.

When the Raging Idiots signed a record deal with Black River Entertainment in the spring of 2015, it was a dream come true for me. I never, ever thought I would be in a band that was on an actual legitimate label. My natural inclination was to immediately suffocate my happiness by imagining all the different ways I was surely going to screw this up. Instead, I took myself out for a chicken-fried steak at Cracker Barrel. I didn't think about whether I was going to succeed or fail. I just enjoyed that steak. And that was it. I had my moment, and I moved on (then I was sure the Raging Idiots were going to fail).

As much as possible I'm trying to enjoy right now, because as my high school football coach Vic Gandolph says, "Every day is a good day."

Now, I know you are thinking, Wait, everyday *really* isn't a good day. No, it's not true in a literal sense. But while I was in Mountain Pine, Coach beat it into our heads that every single day was an opportunity for a good day. While doing up-downs for seemingly hours at a time, Coach would yell "EVERY DAY IS A GOOD DAY!" Trust me, at the time it didn't feel very good.

When I returned to my high school to speak at graduation, Coach Gandolph showed up even though he doesn't work there anymore. He gave me the ball that we had given him my senior year, and we talked for a bit. I told him that it was only recently I understood what he meant by his mantra.

It's all about the choice and the chance that comes every morning when each of us rises to face a new day. Like yesterday, when I received the call that the television talk show, the one for which I survived about forty-five auditions and ten thousand different panels, didn't get picked up for a pilot. It's a bummer that I won't be on TV, but out of the experience I made a new and important friend: Deion Sanders.

Or today, when I woke up at 3 A.M., did the radio show, worked on this book, had a TV production meeting, walked Dusty, went to rehearsal for a sold-out charity show with my band the Raging Idiots, worked out, sound-checked at 4 P.M., walked Dusty again, performed with Carrie Underwood at 7 P.M., did press until 2 A.M., and raised a ton of money for St. Jude.

Right before I go to sleep I'll look up at the Mountain Pine sign—Pop. 772—above my head and know that all I'm allowed to do in my life makes for some pretty long days. Still, I wake up every morning ready to start pushing buttons again.

ACKNOWLEDGMENTS

I'd like to thank Rebecca Paley, who led me through the entire writing process.

Thanks to Carrie Thornton, my editor, for trusting me, guiding me, and most important, for being patient with me through the process. Thanks also to all the crew at HarperCollins and Dey Street Books.

Thanks to my iHeartRadio family. There are lots to name, so I won't even try to list them all.

Bob Pittman, thank you.

Rich Bressler, thank you.

Rod Phillips, thank you.

Jennifer Leimgruber, Julie Talbot, and Darren Davis, thank you. To my manager, Coran Capshaw, who read this book and sternly told me what was worth getting in trouble for and what wasn't, thank you.

To my manager Mary Forrest Findlay, who read this book and told me I was going to get in trouble for everything! Ha ha. Thanks!

To my literary agent, Alan Nevins, and my radio agent, Paul Anderson, I really appreciate you guys. To Jay Shannon, you're always my dude! Thanks to Charlamagne Tha God and Kennedy for being great friends but even greater professional influences.

To Amy, my cohost forever and one of my best friends in life. Thanks for keeping me in rails.

Special thanks to John Mayer for making the album *Continuum*.

Also, a big sad hug to the Counting Crows for making lots of great music that makes me sad.

Thanks to all of the great Nashville artists who I've mentioned in this book. And who have really helped my love for Nashville grow.

I love Arkansas and the Razorbacks.

I love Austin, Texas,

I love my dog, Dusty.

To _____, thanks for marrying me and making me the happiest guy ever. (Still waiting to fill that blank.)

To every listener who has let me ramble on and still continues listening. Without you guys, this wouldn't exist.

#FightGrindRepeat

ABOUT THE AUTHOR

BOBBY BONES hosts *The Bobby Bones Show,* a morning radio program that is in national syndication with Premiere Networks (owned by iHeartRadio). Nationally, it is the biggest country music morning show in America, with an estimated audience of nearly five million listeners. Bobby has appeared in films, and on television and records, and he tours with his band Bobby Bones and The Raging Idiots. He lives in Nashville, Tennessee.